MANHOOD
WITH
MEANING

MANHOOD WITH MEANING

"THE GOD PRINCIPLE"

RICHARD HALVERSON

ZONDERVAN PUBLISHING HOUSE
A DIVISION OF THE ZONDERVAN CORPORATION
GRAND RAPIDS, MICHIGAN

Contents

MANHOOD WITH MEANING

1 ~ Where Do We Go From Here?

Revolution smolders and in its glare is revealed confusion, perplexity, frustration; the bewildering futility of man's efforts for peace which we in our blindness or pride seem so reluctant to admit. Let's look frankly at our position in this enlightened mid-twentieth century.

We know more about child psychology, yet have more juvenile delinquency than ever. Law enforcement has become a science, sociologists have the answers on criminal rehabilitation, yet the crime rate rises steadily.

Yale studies on alcoholism, A.A. working overtime, clinics, medication; yet every hour in the U.S. fifty new alcoholics (1200 daily). Hundreds of books and articles on marriage, clinics and counselors everywhere, yet the divorce rate is ascending.

Unprecedented application of psychology, psychiatry, psychoanalysis and psychotherapy; yet mental hospitals are crowded, mental illness increases, and millions exist on benzedrine, tranquilizers, and sleeping pills. Even the perfecting of astounding new antibiotics seem to trigger new, unfamiliar and mystifying viruses.

America burdened with a growing food surplus, preoccupied with dieting, while half the world never knows the luxury of a full stomach, millions perish of starvation; and the only apparent solution to population explosion is some method of keeping babies from being born.

Diplomacy has become a profession; in high optimism the U.N. was born out of the disillusionment of an abortive League of Nations; yet international relations are more explosive than ever; two world wars in a quarter century; yet, despite unceasing efforts at disarmament, a hysterical race to stockpile suicidal weap-

11

ons. More and more talk about peace; less and less hope for it!

✗ Humanity longs and struggles for freedom, yet half the world languishes under two giant dictatorships and a host of lesser ones; and the monolith of Communism, like a juggernaut rolls over the world.

✗ Technology has united the world as never before; yet it has never been so divided and fragmented: two Germanys, two Koreas, two Chinas, two Vietnams, and an amazing birth rate of new and independent states in Asia and Africa. Incredible progress in technology and science, but the consummate product of that progress constitutes a sickening, relentless threat to our survival.

One step forward, two backward, seems to be history's pattern. Looks like the smarter we are, the farther behind we get. (Read Romans 8:18-25.)

Jesus Christ said, "Apart from me, you can do nothing!" (John 15:5).

2 — Performance vs. Pietism

Today again the church is polarizing around these two *basic facts* of authentic Christian faith.

On one side are those for whom theology is immaterial—who insist that Christianity is just a matter of doing good to others . . .

On the other side are those who take theology seriously—who emphasize evangelism—but who fail to comprehend their Christian responsibility to social sickness and do something about it.

(On both sides are those who force their theology to fit their practice, whose authority, therefore, is their tradition rather than the Bible.)

Christianity certainly involves performance!

At the heart of our Lord's teaching is love . . . which He incarnated.

Love is *meaningless apart from performance* . . . one who professes to love must love his neighbor. Jesus demonstrated the love He taught.

And He insisted—as did the apostles—that *love is central to faith*.

The Bible abounds in exhortations to feed the poor, clothe the naked, care for the afflicted, help the weak, visit those in prison, etc.

Christian faith that does not perform—that is not the incarnation of what it professes—is something less than New Testament Christianity.

Incarnation implies experience. Christian faith is first an experience!

Christianity began as the disciples responded to Jesus Christ—learned of Him—and finally, after Pentecost, experienced Him in their lives.

He had been *with* them during His public ministry . . . He was *in* them after Pentecost.

The work He had done separate from them at first was done in and through them after the Holy Spirit was given.

Performance which does not flow from this Christ-centered personal experience is sub-Christian. At best it is an imitation of Christianity without the reality.

Pietism and performance belong together . . . in that order!

"God is at work in you, both to will and to work for his good pleasure" (Phil. 2:13).

3 — Starving Your Soul?

Are you starving your soul?

You eat three square meals a day—try to get proper rest and exercise for the sake of your body . . .

Do you leave your soul undernourished — weak — anemic?

Bodily health is important . . . but soul health is infinitely more so! ("What will it profit a man if he gains the whole world—and loses his soul?")

Modern man is so easily absorbed in the physical—so prone to be indifferent to the spiritual. He is apt to major in the temporal—ignore the eternal.

Here is the key to much of modern exhaustion and frustration. Man battles to keep the body in shape . . . lets his soul go to pot . . . and wonders why he's petering out!

He feels drained all the time. Wakes up in the morning less rested than when he went to bed. He goes to work because he must—not because He wants to.

Life loses its vitality and drive. It's pale—thin—uninteresting—unchallenging. Living is drudgery—a duty instead of a privilege.

So he goes on the pill and tonic routine—resorts to cocktails for pick-up. But the help is only temporary—he begins to get satisfaction in inverse ration to the amount of pills and tonic and cocktails. Their power to pick up diminishes fast!

Finally the cure becomes as dull and boring and monotonous as the disease.

The man is fed up!

His *body is saturated* with attention . . . his *soul is dried up* with neglect.

He's put everything on that which is destined to rot in a grave . . . abandoned that which was meant to live forever!

What kind of a fool is man anyway?

And to compound the problem, he justifies his neglect by letting himself be talked out of faith. He argues himself out of belief in Christ and eternity . . . but deep inside him his soul cries out for recognition—languishes for attention.

Get wise, man! You were made for fellowship with God! LIFE BEGINS WITH CHRIST!

"This is eternal life, that they know thee the only true God, and Jesus Christ whom thou hast sent" (John 17:3).

4 — The Sacrifice of Thanksgiving

"The sacrifice of thanksgiving . . ." (Ps. 116:17). How does one offer such a sacrifice?

It means to thank God when one does not feel like it!

It means to thank God when there seems to be nothing for which to be thankful.

It means to thank God when circumstances are absolutely contrary to the giving of thanks!

It means to thank God with the will rather than the emotions.

It is to give God thanks for what He is rather than what He gives!

Thank God for Himself rather than His gifts!

Thanking God just for obvious blessings and benefits and gifts is to miss life's choicest reasons for thankfulness. In retrospect, often life's trials bring the chiefest blessings

    —life's testings the deepest benefits

    —life's tragedies the greatest triumphs!

Thanking God whether circumstances are favorable or not; thanking God when circumstances are unfavorable; this is to recognize God for what He is.

To be thankful to God for the fact of His overruling goodness and providence in all things.

To be thankful to God for Himself, for His integrity, His faithfulness, His unfailing love!

Small the man who thanks God only for what God gives!

Blind the man who measures thankfulness by the benefits of God rather than the God who benefits!

Thanking God for Himself is the sacrifice of thanksgiving because it is for God Himself alone, not for what He does or gives. It is the sacrifice of thanksgiving because it is more than emotional sentimentality; it is an action of the dedicated will.

15

Offer God the sacrifice of thanksgiving, daily.

"We know that in everything God works for good with those who love him, who are called according to his purpose" (Rom. 8:28).

5 — Me!

You're going to meet an old man someday! Down the road ahead — ten, twenty, thirty years — waiting there for you. You'll be catching up with him.

What kind of an old man are you going to meet? That's a rather significant question.

He may be a seasoned, soft, gracious fellow — a gentleman that has grown old gracefully—surrounded by hosts of friends . . . friends who call him blessed because of what his life has meant to them.

He may be a bitter, disillusioned, dried-up, cynical old buzzard—without a good word for anyone—soured, friendless and alone.

The kind of an old man you will meet depends entirely on yourself. Because that old man will be you. He'll be the composite of everything you do, say, think —today, tomorrow. His mind will be set in a mold you have made by your attitudes. His heart will be turning out what you've been putting in.

Every little thought—every deed goes into this old man. *He'll be exactly what you make him* — nothing more — nothing less. It's up to you. You'll have no one else to credit or blame.

Every day in every way you are becoming more and more like yourself. Amazing—but true! You're getting to look more like yourself—think more like yourself— talk more like yourself. You're becoming yourself more and more.

Live only in terms of what you're getting out of life —the old man gets smaller, drier, harder, crabbier, more self-centered.

Open your life to others, think in terms of what you

can give, your contribution to life—the old man grows larger, softer, kindlier, greater.

A point to remember is that *these things don't always tell immediately.* But they'll show up sooner than you think. These little things—so unimportant now—attitudes, goals, ambitions, desires—they're adding up inside—where you can't see them . . . crystallizing in your heart and mind. Some day they'll harden into that old man—nothing will be able to soften or change them.

Time to take care of that old man is right now—today, this week. Examine his motives, attitudes, goals. Check up on him. Work him over while he's still plastic—still in a formative condition. Day comes awfully soon when it's too late. The hardness sets in—worse than paralysis—character crystallizes, sets, jells. That's the finish.

Any wise businessman takes inventory regularly. His merchandise isn't half as important as he is. Better take a bit of personal inventory, too. We all need it—in the light of Christ and His Word. You'll be much more likely to meet a splendid, old fellow at the proper time—the fellow you'd like to be.

"Do not be deceived; God is not mocked, for *whatever a man sows,* that he will also reap" (Gal. 6:7).

"The path of the righteous is like the light of dawn, which shines brighter and brighter until full day" (Prov. 4:18).

6 ~ True Testimony

The trouble with so many testimonies is that they are little personal success stories couched in pious language . . .

Such testimonies have done as much as any single thing to kill the efficacy of witness in our contemporary world!

Modern man is unimpressed because the world is filled with men who have achieved success the hard way—without any need for faith or any personal reference to Jesus Christ . . .

He understands little—and respects less—the man who had to "use God" to "make a bundle."

Elton Trueblood, in his book *The Company of the Committed,* reminds us that authentic Christian testimony has two aspects: personal and historical.

The historical aspect, the fact of Jesus Christ—His life, His deeds, His words . . .

The personal aspect, the relevance of this historical fact to one's own life.

Authentic testimony witnesses to the fact that Jesus Christ has proved to me He is what He said He was—and He has done for me what He said He would do.

Authentic personal testimony says in effect, *Jesus Christ has made good on His promises!*

True testimony confirms the integrity of Jesus Christ in the experience of the man giving it.

Not uncommonly the most vital witness testifies to the relevance of Christ in the midst of difficulty and failure. How Christ helped a man handle failure speaks to most men!

Men prosper without God! This, in fact, is one of the deepest issues wrestled with in the Bible: Why do wicked men prosper?

The Bible makes it clear that "God sends the rain on the just and on the unjust." He is utterly impartial with many of His blessings.

Success stories do not honor Jesus Christ!

Testimonies to His love and forgiveness—His mercy and grace in one's daily living — His enablement for duty and virtue—His triumph in trials—His adequacy for the daily grind. . . . These witness to His greatness —His reality—His relevance!

"I can do all things through Christ who strengthens me . . ."—Paul.

7 — The Faithfulness of God

There are times when all a man has to go on is the integrity of God.

But that is all a man needs!

God makes the difference in any situation: no matter how bleak, how discouraging, how hopeless circumstances appear to be.

"Nothing is too hard for God!"

Any man, with God, is a majority anywhere, anytime, in any situation. The man who counts on the integrity of God is an indomitable, invincible man. He may be down for the moment, but he is never out.

Realizing the integrity of God puts resilience, perseverance, "bounce-back" in him.

He may not know what the future holds, but he is absolutely sure of the *One* who is in charge of the future.

He may not see his way out of circumstances that have hemmed him in and cut him off from escape, but he knows God is not hemmed in or cut off.

God is never victimized by circumstances. He is always the master. So is the man that trusts in God.

He may not be able to see through or around, but he can look *up!*

A man may be at the end of his rope because of personal failure and defeat, feel that he is worthless and there is no use going on, but he knows God will turn every failure into triumph by the alchemy of His grace.

He never takes failure or defeat as final, but always as part of the process.

He knows they become a stepping stone to future success for the man who stands on the unfailing, changeless integrity of God.

A man may not "feel" God, may not be aware of

His presence, but he knows God is there because He has promised never to leave.

He does not trust his own sense of God, he trusts God's promise to be there, always:

Because the sun is behind a cloud does not change the fact that it is there, and though circumstances may obscure God's presence, the *fact is* He is there!

Gloom and depression do not affect God's integrity.

Circumstances change, but *God never changes!* A man can count on this, completely!

God's integrity stands! Others may fail, the world may blow up, heaven and earth may crumble; God stands, unchallengeable, inflexible, enduring, everlasting.

And because it stands the man who trusts in God will also stand.

He may weaken, but he will hold.

He may fail, but he is never a failure.

He may lose a battle, but he is absolutely certain to win the war!

"If God is for us, who is against us?" (Rom. 8:31).

". . . I am sure that neither death, nor life, nor angels, nor principalities, nor things present, nor things to come, nor powers, . . . will be able to separate us from the love of God in Christ Jesus our Lord" (Rom. 8:38, 39).

8 — God's Remedy

What I see in the church today is a massive diversion from primary to secondary issues.

The secondary issues are profound . . . but they are secondary!

They are the effects of which the cause is being largely neglected.

One man, for example, says "poverty is the disease." Very well, the genesis of the disease has been isolated by Christ — it is the depravity of man — and He has provided a remedy—His crucifixion and resurrection.

Poverty will never be eradicated if the cause is ignored . . . any more than poliomyelitis would have been eliminated by building iron lungs.

Yet today we see the church, the only institution with an adequate remedy, largely preoccupied with the symptoms—neglecting the mandate left by Jesus Christ — which mandate is the divine solution to all social disease.

It is as if teachers were to stop educating in order to devote themselves to the resolution of racial tension, poverty and urban blight.

As if manufacturers and farmers closed their farms and factories and devoted themselves to social action.

As if the medical profession ceased from its ministry of healing for the sake of involvement "where the action is."

If the apostolic faith is the criterion for the church, then the propagation of the Gospel is primary for it is *God's means of reconciliation between man and Himself,* hence between men whether the alienation be racial, economic, or social.

Neglecting the Gospel in the attempt to reconcile men is self-defeating!

Of course, there is division of labor in the church as well as elsewhere. In the economy of God, disciples are endowed with diverse gifts, sent to diverse places, to do diverse works among diverse peoples.

Some are called to social action and would be irresponsible if they did not fulfill that obligation (all Christians are called to social responsibility within their areas of personal influence).

On the other hand, all Christians are sent as witnesses of the Gospel of Christ and when they fail to give priority to this task, social action and social responsibility fail of their goals.

"I am under obligation both to Greeks and to barbarians . . . I am eager to preach the gospel . . . it is the power of God for salvation to every one who has faith . . ." (Rom. 1:14-16).

9 — Consider Grace

Have you ever seriously considered grace? . . . The grace of God? Understand but slightly the significance of God's grace—it can revitalize your life!

God's grace is *inexhaustible!* You can't use it up—wear it out! It is like the air you breathe: no matter how much you take in—or how often—or how many breathe at the same time—there is always plenty left.

It is *sufficient* for any need in your life! Don't let this slip by too easily! That means that God's provision for you anticipates way ahead — and more than covers—any need you may have . . . whether material or spiritual.

It is *immediate* in its availability. Like the air—God's grace surrounds you—waiting to be let in. The split second you admit your need, open your life—it floods your soul with immeasurable supply.

Like sound waves: the air is full of them — but you've got to tune in on your radio to hear the music. You miss God's grace because you do not tune in. Really—no attitude in life is more stupid than to refuse to tune in on God.

God's grace is *constant!* It has no variable element in it. He is "the same yesterday, today and forever." He never changes. You can depend on God—always, anytime.

God's grace is *continuous!* It never stops. It is always there—right at the door of your heart—flowing, pushing, wooing, waiting . . . for you to let it in.

It is *all-forgiving!* This is the supreme expression of God's grace. "Christ died for our sins according to the scriptures." In the cross, God revealed the infinity of His love. God's grace forgives all sin—on the basis of His Son's sacrifice on the cross.

22

All but one! It cannot cover the sin of refusal! Refuse to receive God's grace—it will not help you. Any more than the air will help you if you refuse to breathe . . . any more than you can hear the radio program if you refuse to tune in.

God's grace is *free!* What an understatement! You can't earn it—you can't deserve it. If you earn it—if you are worthy of it—it is not grace. In fact, grace means this—unmerited favor. This is the key! Some men miss the point—in their pride, they try to earn God's favor.

One man refused the Gospel on the grounds that it was free! In his puffed-up, self-reliance he dismissed it with these words: "I believe in paying my way. I don't need anyone's help." His false self-sufficiency was his greatest enemy. Actually, it was stubborn pride! Wonder whom he pays for the air he breathes—and how much?

"As your days, so shall your strength be" (Deut. 33:25). "Where sin increased, grace abounded all the more" (Rom. 5:20). "My God will supply every need of yours according to his riches in glory in Christ Jesus" (Phil. 4:19). That's grace. Receive it!

10 — A Time to Wait

"Stand still . . . !"

Under the circumstances that command must have sounded insane.

Stand still? With an enemy horde driving in for the kill? That was precisely the command Moses issued to Israel.

Humanly speaking it was gross foolishness; but it was the wisdom of God!

Israel was really cornered. Her situation was hopeless: Red Sea before her, armies of Egypt sweeping in from the rear, impassable mountains and desert on her flanks.

Things couldn't have been worse.

In this predicament Moses commanded, "Stand still!"

"Stand still and be slaughtered? Stand still and be mowed down by the heartless warriors of Pharaoh?" reasoned some of the Hebrews; and following "common sense" they fled into the teeth of disaster.

They drowned in the sea or perished in the wilderness, if they were not brutally slaughtered by the Egyptians.

Those spared were those who heeded Moses' counsel: "Stand still and see the salvation of the Lord."

(Whoever would have thought of parting the Red Sea so Israel could walk through on dry ground? *God did!*)

God's ways are utterly beyond man's inventions.

"As high as the heavens above the earth are God's ways above man's . . ."

Human alternatives are few, but God is never limited to human alternatives!

He has ways of which man has never dreamed. The God of creation can create alternatives if necessary.

For this reason "hopeless" is not rightly a Christian word. It should be stricken from the Christian's vocabulary.

A man may have exhausted the possibilities for a way out of a complex dilemma, but the situation is never hopeless.

"God is able!"

Much that man calls "common sense" is nothing more than a last resort tactic. Having wracked his brain for solutions, and running out of possibilities, he is inclined to do "just anything." Figuring doing something is better than doing nothing, he tries "anything," which often leads to greater complications or disaster.

When things look hopeless the man who waits confidently on God will discover God has unthinkable answers. The intelligent way is God's way. It is always too soon to despair! When circumstances are impossible, that is the time to . . .

"Stand still, and see the salvation of the Lord!" (Exod. 14:13, KJV).

11 — For Laymen

Let the layman be the layman!

He is not supposed to be a carbon copy of the pastor.

He was not meant to be a second team man who substitutes for the pastor occasionally.

(Nor was he meant to sit on the bench part of the time—the game demands every player all of the time.)

He was not meant to be a semi-pro in the work of the church doing the same things the pastor is called to do.

Herein lies the breakdown with much so-called "lay training."

It's designed to produce a part-time assistant minister minus ordination.

(One church, after an elaborate training program, actually instituted a special ordination for those who completed the training.)

In the economy of God, the church needs non-clergy as well as clergy . . .

And the role of the non-clergy is as significant as that of the clergy.

One is not superior to the other . . . the only difference is functional.

The division of labor introduced by Christ into His church cannot be improved upon. It *involves every member* and suffers when any member fails to function.

This does not mean a layman should not preach— that depends upon the gifts with which he is endowed by the Spirit of God.

But it does mean that his gifts and calling are integral to the life of the church and its work in the world whether he preaches or not.

25

Nor does it mean that he is called to devote his spare time to "church work."

The work of the church is not what is done for the church—for the religious establishment . . . the work of the church lies *outside and beyond the institution* of the church.

The work of the church is in the world—where the layman is all the time. It is there Christ has placed him to do what he does there all the time to the glory of God as a minister and messenger of reconciliation (2 Cor. 5:14-21).

"And his gifts were that some should be apostles . . . for the equipment of the saints, for the work of ministry . . ." (Eph. 4:11, 12).

12 – God Leads

God uses many means to lead a man . . .

Important thing is that He leads!

God may engineer circumstances so that a man has no alternatives and there's only one way to go.

He may "speak" through a passage of Scripture or through the conversation of a friend or through a sermon . . .

But the final test is inward — what might be called intuition.

This is the "still small voice" within.

Assuming a man's openness to the will of God—his intuition can be trusted.

"Commit your work to the Lord and your plans will be established," wrote Solomon (Prov. 16:3).

Paul the apostle speaks of having the "mind of God."

Whatever other means God may use to direct, He will establish a man's thoughts.

God's Spirit within checks or inhibits a man one way or another.

"Where the Spirit of the Lord is, there is liberty" (2 Cor. 3:17).

The man who is seeking to know and do God's will may trust the gentle inner restraint or release of the Spirit.

Spiritual intuition will not go contrary to the will of God as revealed in Scripture, however. God does not contradict the revelation He has given in the Bible . . .

The Spirit speaks consistently with the Word.

The decisive person has more than logic going for him . . .

The man who submits to the will of God and depends upon the guidance of God will be a decisive person.

"Trust in the Lord with all your heart, and do not rely on your own insight. In all your ways acknowledge him, and he will make straight your paths" (Prov. 3:5, 6).

13 — Hero in the Home

What kind of a man are you at home?

Are you a husband—father—friend?

Or are you a tin god—a little Napoleon—a dictator —a strutting boss?

When you get home, do you expect the little world there to revolve around you like the earth around the sun?

Does your family dread your arrival . . . or anticipate it eagerly—joyfully?

A man can be a big success in business . . . and fail miserably at home.

He may be a big shot downtown . . . and a big fake with his family.

Home is where greatness really shows up!

Do you expect more from your children than you give them?

Are you telling them how to act . . . instead of showing them?

Do you demand their silence — and then interrupt

when they are speaking as though what they say doesn't matter . . . your words are the only ones important?

Do you demand their respect . . . or earn it?

Some men are more interested in bowling than in their boy . . . in golf than their girl. They spend more time at the club than with their children . . . show more interest in their work than in their wife.

"One father is worth more than 100 schoolteachers" . . . but men have to be fathers—not just providers.

It is a truism that the home is the basic unit of society . . . that as the home, so goes the nation.

What kind of a home are you making?

Here is a major tragedy in our modern world: adult men, successful in business, popular in their circle — prominent, level-headed, sharp men — get away with things in their private club, and other places, which when done by their boys are labeled "juvenile delinquency."

Where do these boys get their ideas? Not from skid row! The smoother — more suave — classier the man . . . the more appealing his misdeeds to the boy.

"Men of distinction" stuff! Tommy-rot!

It would be humorous—if not so pitifully tragic!

Plain fact is just because a thing isn't hurting you doesn't mean it is right for you!

Think this over! It may not hurt you . . . but some boy is watching you . . . maybe your boy.

And you'd be surprised what he notices . . . the little things he picks up! The "social drink"—gambling at the club—obscene story in the locker room—foul language which passes so smoothly in "elite" circles.

It carries a whale of an appeal for young lives. They go for it! It's a "natural" for them.

So they copy it!

You are a hero to your boy, Dad!

He's watching you closely.

He's studying your life.

He mimics you . . . wants to grow up like you.

What kind of a man are you giving him for a standard?

That's important!

"Husbands, love your wives, as Christ loved the church and gave himself up for her . . . Fathers, do not provoke your children to anger, but bring them up in the discipline and instruction of the Lord" (Eph. 5:25; 6:4).

14 — Daily In-put

That incredible computer between your ears . . .

What a remarkable instrument!

The equivalent in electronic equipment would fill a structure larger than the Empire State Building.

It is inconceivably delicate in its receiving and memory systems . . . infinitely refined by comparison with man's most sophisticated machines.

Its daily in-put is astounding.

Second by second it records impressions fed in through the senses . . .

Programming the responses you will make when life demands answers.

Question is, What are you putting into this fantastic system?

What are you looking at — listening to — tasting — touching . . . ?

What are you reading—what kind of pictures engage your attention—what programs on radio and TV? How do you spend your leisure?

Hours in every day you are responsible for the input . . .

You are programming your answers to life.

"Garbage in—garbage out!"

"Blessed is the man who walks not in the counsel of the wicked, nor stands in the way of sinners, nor sits in the seat of the scoffers; but his delight is in the law of the Lord, and on his law he meditates day and night. He is like a tree planted by streams of water, that yields its fruit in its season, and its leaf does not wither. In all that he does, he prospers" (Ps. 1:1-3).

"The good man out of his good treasure brings forth good, and the evil man out of his evil treasures brings forth evil" (Matt. 12:35).

15 — No Substitute

"Blood is the magic gift of life . . .

"There is no substitute!"

Thus a local Red Cross chapter announced its drive for more blood donors.

The accuracy of that statement is precisely the point of Good Friday.

"The life of the flesh is in the blood" (Lev. 17:11).

Millenniums before medical science discovered the life-giving, life-carrying nature of blood, Moses the prophet spoke of it in the Bible.

Nearly 500 times the Bible refers to blood—because *blood is at the center* of the message which the Bible carries.

It was the blood on the doorposts of the homes of Israel that spared them death one black day in Egypt . . . and Passover has been celebrated annually since in commemoration of that escape from death by blood.

"When I see the blood, I will pass over" (Exod. 12:13).

Blood sacrifice was made twice daily by the priests of Israel for the sins of the people.

On that great day — the Day of Atonement — the whole complicated liturgy centered in that moment when the high priest, bearing the blood of the sacrifice, entered through the veil into the Holy of Holies, where only he could enter once a year.

And as the record of the Old Testament unfolds, it becomes progressively clearer that One is to rise out of Israel—a Messiah, whose blood is to be shed in a fulfillment which all the bloody past of Israel's sacrifices prefigured.

He was to be the "suffering servant" who was to "bear our sins in his own body on the tree"—by whose "stripes we are healed."

Jesus Christ died on the cross for man's sins — *for your sins!*

That's what Good Friday is all about!

16 ~ God Is

Every man has a god!
Even the atheist!

He believes in No-god . . . often is more zealous—more religious about his belief in No-god than some men who believe in God.

It is not easy to have faith in No-god! Such a faith is held in the face of overwhelming evidence to the contrary.

In fact, the only thing that "saves face" for the atheist is the fact of God's existence. No one would take an atheist seriously if there were no God. Anymore than you would a man who made a big deal out of proving there is no Santa Claus.

Why pay attention to a man who labors to disprove what is nonexistent?

GOD IS . . . therefore the atheist is not shadow-boxing —not beating the air. He's conducting a real war against a real Opponent. The fact of God's existence is what gives the atheist status!

Real question is not whether a man believes in God or not . . . but *what kind of a god does he serve?*

One man serves the god mammon: Money is everything! The whole weight of his life is thrown into the acquisition of wealth. More he gets—more he wants. Enough is never! Mammon is a hard taskmaster — a merciless tyrant. It has destroyed many.

31

Another puts pleasure first—follows a giddy—shallow — senseless round of froth. He takes pleasure wherever he finds it—hungrily devours it like a starved animal tearing at a cadaver.

Tragedy is that it takes more and more pleasure to get less and less satisfaction. The point of diminishing returns is reached quickly. Authentic delight decreases in inverse ratio to increased effort. Pitiful pay-off is a hollow life—emptiness—a bubble.

Still another serves the god fame or power or prestige . . . or the worst tyrant of all, the god *self* . . . and inevitably reaps what he sows.

Thing is this: Man becomes like his god! He grows into the image of that which he worships!

The wise man serves the true God—the God of our Lord and Savior Jesus Christ.

What kind of a god do you serve?

"This is eternal life, that they know thee the only true God, and Jesus Christ whom thou hast sent" (Jesus in John 17:3).

17 — Time for Repentance

Recently in a TV comedy hour, one of the laugh routines was the deliberate, total destruction of an automobile by a group with sledge hammers. Gleefully, accompanied by music with the contemporary sound, beat and lyrics, they reduced the car to junk in minutes.

It was a vivid, sickening portrayal of a symptom of this age . . .

Contempt for property!

A symptom dangerously common among youth.

There is no rational justification for it—it is irresponsible and vicious—no simple, single explanation can account for it.

But whatever else it is—it is a judgment upon our materialism!

For years affluent parents—indoctrinated with the philosophy of permissiveness—have been "buying off" their youth with things.

"We gave him everything," is the pathetic defense of bewildered parent after parent in conference with counselor or police . . .

By which they mean they gave him everything money could buy . . . everything but love — everything but themselves—everything but spiritual direction.

They reared him in a spiritual and moral vacuum— nurtured him in a climate of nihilism—taught him to believe in Nothing.

By precept and example we parents have convinced our youth that money and things are everything—that position and wealth and status are the goals to be achieved.

And the kids have had it!

It has been estimated that there are seventeen million American youth with absolutely *no religious influence* in their lives.

We are beginning to reap as we have sown . . .

It is *time for repentance!*

"Beware that thou forget not the Lord thy God, in not keeping his commandments . . . Lest when thou hast eaten and are full, and hast built goodly houses, and dwell therein; And when thy herds and thy flocks multiply, and thy silver and thy gold is multiplied . . . Then thine heart be lifted up, and thou forget the Lord thy God . . . And thou say in thy heart, My power and the might of mine hand hath gotten me this wealth . . . I testify against you this day that ye shall surely perish" (Deut. 8:11-19, KJV).

18 — The Healing in Hardness

What kind of a man you are depends entirely on how you take hard knocks, difficulties, defeats when they come.

Every man has them; how he reacts to them is an index to his character, the quality of the man.

Do you grumble or growl when things get a bit tough?

Do you whine or are you determined to win?

Are you the victim or the victor of your circumstances?

Are you a complainer or a creator?

Hardships make the man, and they show up the weakling.

"Reality is only realized by tests! What do you know of a ship on a still day, or a soldier on dress parade, or a surgeon at his dinner table? But give the ship a whirlwind, the soldier a battle, the surgeon a swift opportunity when friends are breathless, then what they are worth comes out."

What a man is like when things go dead against him, that is the test!

The last ten feet of a race, the last thirty seconds of a game, the last bell in the fight; these things reveal the truth about a man.

Anyone can look good when things go right!

Anyone can make an impression when circumstances break his way, when things go smoothly, well-oiled.

Anyone can click then.

The real man knows how to operate against odds.

Consider these facts from Lincoln's life: 1831, failed in business. 1832, defeated for Legislature. 1838, defeated for elector. 1843, defeated for Congress. 1848, defeated for Senate. 1856, defeated for Vice-president; 1860, President of the USA.

"Difficulties, defeats are like exercise. Just as exercise develops muscles, difficulties develop character, give it a chance to expand and grow. The business world is a place of conflict, a place of gains and losses, ups and downs. It is not a pleasant, comfortable office where you sit at a big desk and are smiled at by pretty girls and flattered by executives. Business warfare is not a matter of signing checks and filling in forms. It is a matter of will-power and tenacity and resistance. If a man wants to be a leader he must prove that he does not break under pressure."

A frog was caught in a deep rut in a road, and in spite of the help of his friends, he could not get out. They finally left him there in despair. Next day, one of his friends saw him, chipper as you please, and no longer in the rut. "What are you doing here?" asked the friend. "I thought you couldn't get out." "I couldn't," replied the frog. "But a truck came along the road, and I had to."

"Count it all joy . . . when you meet various trials, for you know that the testing of your faith produces steadfastness" (James 1:2).

19 — Needed: the Gospel

"If religious books are not widely circulated among the masses in this country, and the people do not become religious, I do not know what is to become of us as a nation.

"And the thought is one to cause solemn reflection on the part of every patriot and Christian.

"If truth be not diffused, error will be;

"If God and His Word are not known and received, the devil and his works will gain the ascendancy;

"If the evangelical volume does not reach every hamlet, the pages of a corrupt and licentious literature will;

"If the power of the Gospel is not felt through the length and breadth of the land, anarchy and misrule, degradation and misery, corruption and darkness, will reign without mitigation or end."

Daniel Webster was not "talking through his hat" when he uttered those words . . .

He was prophetic!

The truth which diffused the culture which produced the men who founded America has been replaced . . .

Today the *error of secularism* and scientism and nihilism and materialism is diffused throughout our culture.

The Gospel is not "felt through the length and breadth of the land . . ."

Instead there is spiritual anarchy and moral relativism . . .

And pages of "corrupt and licentious literature" fill our bookshops.

I can hear the derisive laughter of some of our social-religious engineers as they read this . . . but they offer no solution to the increasing erosion and disintegration of our society — they offer no remedy for the malignancy of the human heart that begets social destruction.

The plain fact is that there is *only one remedy in history*—that is the Gospel which Webster declared must be "felt through the length and breadth of the land."

"I am not ashamed of the gospel: it is the power of God for salvation to every one who has faith . . ." (Rom. 1:16).

"The blood of Jesus his Son cleanses us from all sin" (1 John 1:7).

20 ~ Security ~ In Christ

Change is inevitable . . .

Wherever—whenever Christ touches life!

(Not change for its own sake . . . but change which transforms life, conforming it to the divine pattern.)

To resist change is to resist Christ!

Think how Christ changed things when He entered history in His incarnation . . .

Think of the radical, revolutionary alterations He brought—

Which is why the religionists resisted him.

Christ threatened all they held dear.

He was a threat to the traditions of the conservatives—the Pharisees . . .

He was a threat to the position of the liberals—the Sadducees . . .

He was a threat to the vested interests of the clergy . . . institutionalized religion had a huge stake in the status quo.

So when Christ persisted . . . they killed Him!

Why do men fear change?

Because *their security is in the status quo*—and men love security . . . it is like a god to them.

The cult of the status quo is idolatrous.

Hence, Christ's plain, hard, devastating words: "No man can serve two masters; for either he will hate the one and love the other, or he will be devoted to the one and despise the other. You cannot serve God and mammon" (Matt. 6:24).

If security is found in the status quo—men will hate God—despise God . . . whatever their pious facade.

Paradoxically—true security is found only in Christ. "You must be born again!"

That's essential change in the radical ultimate!

21 — Time Is Priceless

Kill time!

Reckless, unjustifiable homicide!

Four men chatted in the lounge of a DC-7 as it landed at a west coast airport. They had a problem; what to do with two and a half hours before their continuing flight was scheduled to depart. Several plans were discussed and eliminated as impractical. There was not enough time to get into the city and return. "Well, we've got two and a half hours to kill," they concluded, as the four engines died and the ramp swung up to the plane.

How often do you suppose those same men had

grumbled about the lack of time? ("Not enough time" is such a common American gripe.) Yet their range of interests was so limited that they were frustrated by a plan to capitalize on 150 precious minutes. Apparently lacking imagination to do anything constructive, they decided to kill it!

No gift for man's use is more precious than time. It cannot be hoarded. The one way to save it is to spend it, wisely, by investing it in constructive pursuits. Wasted, it can never be recovered.

How often a man neglects Bible reading or prayer, or companionship with his family, or service to his community or church, on the grounds of the lame and transparent excuse, "not enough time"? How many worthwhile projects have been left undone because a man was "too busy"? Yet with what consummate ease has each of us "killed time" again and again.

God made no mistake when He appointed man steward over twenty-four hours a day. Man does not need more time; he must handle with delicate care this priceless possession. It is not how much time a man puts in; it is how much he puts into the time that matters.

"Look carefully, not as fools, but as wise, redeeming the time, because the days are evil" (Eph. 5:15, 16).

22 — Make Haste Slowly

"The hurrier I go, the behinder I get!"

The plight of the man who lets enthusiasm victimize him.

He doesn't possess zeal; zeal possesses him!

Mistaking hysteria for urgency, a man may run off in all directions at once; his energy and effort so diffused that its force is spent long before a purpose is achieved. Like hitting a target with a head of cabbage. Acting in haste, without taking time to let his zeal soak in prayer and counsel, his projects peter out; abortive because premature!

Without the seasoning, maturing process of prayerful reflection, ideas, no matter how good, generally lack the strength of fulfillment. Patience is more than a human virtue; it is of the Spirit of God, and it is of the essence of Christian greatness.

Let the idea spawn; it will produce offspring.

Heed the counsel of one of the most profound devotional writers. He knew the "mind of Christ" and speaks out of deep, seasoned, tempered wisdom. "Never act in a panic, nor allow man to dictate to thee. Calm thyself and be still. Force thyself into the quiet of thy closet until thy pulse beats normally and the scare has ceased to disturb. When thou art most eager to act is the time when thou wilt make the most pitiable mistakes. Do not say in thine heart what thou wilt or wilt not do, but wait upon God until He makes known His way. So long as that way is hidden, it is clear that there is no need of action; and that He accounts Himself responsible for all the result of keeping thee where thou art" (F. B. Meyer).

"They who wait for the Lord shall renew their strength, they shall mount up with wings like eagles, they shall run and not be weary, they shall walk and not faint" (Isa. 40:31).

23 — First Things First

Second-hand faith is an anomaly!

Christian faith cannot be inherited, though its benefits are . . .

Which is the crux of moral disintegration.

The modern American who enjoys all the benefits of Christian faith while at the same time ignoring that faith is like a prodigal son, who having long since used up the interest of a father's inheritance is now squandering the capital.

And to compound the problem, he is making no spiritual and moral deposit for subsequent generations . . . his legacy to his progeny is spiritual bankruptcy!

Such men are spiritual parasites—living off the benefits of the faith of former generations—depleting the moral capital of their generation—and robbing posterity of the benefits so richly enjoyed by themselves.

One evidence of this present-day spiritual profligacy is the fact that men take the benefits of religious dedication for granted.

Our civilization is not automatic! It was born out of a deep and abiding faith in God—a sense of accountability to Him—an awareness of His overruling providence in the affairs of men.

Moral purity is the fruit of which spiritual dedication is the root! Reject the root—loss of the fruit is inevitable!

"The political and social practices of our civilization derive from their Christian content—and they will not long survive unless they are replenished by that faith . . . practice unsupported by belief is a wasting asset" (Arnold J. Toynbee).

". . . reason and experience both forbid us to expect that national morality can prevail in exclusion of religious principle" (George Washington).

"The terrible things that are happening in some parts of the world are due to the fact that political and social practices have been separated from spiritual content" (John Foster Dulles).

"Many laymen are living in the twilight of their parents' religion. When the twilight is past, they will be in complete darkness unless they make the vital ideals of their parents a part of their own experiences" (Dr. Arthur L. Bietz, Lynwood, California, from "Incentives," Christian Men, Inc.).

"Seek first his kingdom and his righteousness . . ." (Matt. 6:33).

24 — Born Again

One reason the church is failing today is that *it has so many members who are not kingdom of God men and women!*

They may be active in the church program—regular at worship—involved in the administration of the religious establishment . . .

But they lack kingdom of God qualities.

They have never seen the kingdom of God!

Because they have not been born again and the new birth is prerequisite to the kingdom.

They are unregenerate church people who have never received the life of God which was given in Jesus Christ.

They may be moral, ethical and respectable—at least as far as outward performance is concerned . . .

But inwardly they are governed by prejudice—greed—avarice—pride—jealousy—illicit ambition.

Disdainful of the "hot, disreputable sins," they commit secretly the "cold, respectable sins."

They manage with some success to project a conventional Christian image in public if not in private . . .

But they do not produce kingdom of God conditions in their spheres of influence.

They maintain the status—but not the substance!

They are agents of dispeace rather than peace—bring alienation rather than reconciliation—compound social tension and conflict.

Moderately good people, they deny Christ by their attitude however pious their profession.

They need a radical — revolutionary — personal change. They need to be born again!

Jesus answered, "Unless one is born anew, he cannot see the kingdom of God" (John 3:3).

25 — The Exercise of Faith

He prayed for patience; God sent him tribulation.

He asked for faith; the answer he got was trials.

Christian virtue is not automatic! It involves a process, and the process may sometimes be painful (most learning is painful), but the pay-off is character and integrity. Patience comes through tribulation. Humility is the product of which humiliation is the process.

Character costs!

As one modern advertisement puts it, "Through experience comes faith."

Faith in God may be inactive when circumstances are favorable, and it takes adversity to challenge faith, rouse it, toughen it. Like muscle, faith grows strong and supple with exercise. Easy living leaves faith flaccid, soft, pale.

Like the alternate firing and cooling that temper steel making it hard and tough, difficulties and reverses harden and toughen the Christian.

Men who have been tried in the fire do not crack under strain.

They may give, which is the secret of tensile strength, but they do not break!

Do not be surprised the way God answers your prayers. You can always trust God's answers.

"Count it all joy, my brethren, when you meet various trials, for you know that the testing of your faith produces steadfastness. And let steadfastness have its full effect, that you may be perfect and complete, lacking in nothing" (James 1:2-4).

". . . we rejoice in our sufferings, knowing that suffering produces endurance, and endurance produces character . . ." (Rom. 5:3).

26 — Willing to Believe

Man's will is crucial to faith.

In a most precise sense man believes what he wants to believe.

His intellect may be involved, but it is not primary.

He may rationalize his belief—or unbelief—to justify it, but faith is not primarily a rational matter.

Not that it is irrational . . . it is beyond reason.

For example—here's a man who says he can believe nothing that is not measurable therefore he has faith only in material things.

Yet he believes in love—and love cannot be measured . . .

He believes in joy and sorrow—and they cannot be measured.

He trusts people without subjecting them to scientific tests and measuring their integrity.

In fact, he lives by faith in a hundred little ways each day: faith in those who cook his food—faith in the one who promises to meet him for an appointment—faith in chairs upon which he unquestioningly puts his weight.

Much of his life is spent in acts which involve uncritical trust . . . but he will not believe the Bible—will not trust Jesus Christ.

Not because such faith is irrational . . . but *because he does not want to believe.* He refuses to believe.

There is none so blind as him who will not see . . .

Which is why unbelief is a moral issue . . . it is rejection!

Jesus said, "*If any man will* do God's will, he shall know . . ."

In order to know, one must be willing.

"This is the judgment, that the light has come into the world, and men loved darkness rather than light . . . and does not come to the light" (John 3:19, 20).

43

27 — Misplaced Trust

War begets war!

"You have plowed iniquity," wrote the prophet Hosea . . .

"You have reaped injustice . . .

"You have eaten the fruit of lies.

"Because you have *trusted in your chariots* and in the multitude of your warriors . . .

"Therefore the tumult of war shall rise among your people . . .

"And all your fortresses shall be destroyed."

Ponder the statement—". . . you have trusted in your chariots."

The issue is not the instruments of war . . . the issue is putting one's trust in them.

This is the bottom issue of history—where does man put his trust?

The divine order is trust in God.

Refuse to trust God—all trust will be misplaced.

The man who will not trust in God—who trusts in man and his ingenuity and exploits—will end up *trusting neither God nor man.*

Failure to orient life around trust in God results in the breakdown of trust all down the line.

It is written large in history that no nation—no empire—no kingdom was ever able to perpetuate itself by depending upon military might.

Our nation is no exception!

On our coins we profess "In God we trust."

When we begin to take seriously that profession, we can begin to look forward to the fruits of peace.

"All who take the sword will perish by the sword" (Matt. 26:52).

28 — Toughness Takes Tempering

Rugged times prove the metal in the man, knock the whine out of him, toughen him.

Saw a movie the other day, story of a new automobile from planning board stage. Picture took us through all the preliminary operations; tons of paper work, full-size clay model, hand-made working model, tooling, assembly. Last phase was the proving grounds. The model was put through the most rugged tests from desert heat to sub-zero cold, wet and dry, rough and smooth, before it was ready to market. Those incredibly rugged tests were not designed to wreck the car, but to make it.

In the economy of God, rugged days will serve only to make the Christian man, strengthen him, temper him, season and mature him. And God's grace is always sufficient for the testing process. Steel has a peculiar faculty: when it is hardest, it is brittle! When it is toughest, it is soft! To be workable it must have a balance of hardness and toughness. To be useful it must be tempered. That means a rugged process under intense heat.

Men are like that. They need to be tempered. Being hard is not enough. Brittle men crack under pressure; they need to be pliable too, yet not soft; flexible, yet not wishy washy. Engineers call it "tolerance." They build into a structure the right amount of give and take, the right amount of response to stress and strain. For safety's sake they must eliminate rigidity. Watch the wing of a large plane in flight. Sometimes it looks like it will fall off. It won't! It is built that way, built to yield a bit. Its strength lies in its ability to take pressure. Or the tree that gives a bit with the wind, it is still there, strong as ever. The tree that refuses to yield splits, cracks, falls.

Big men are not big accidentally. They get that way by taking pressure, stress and strain. They have "tolerance." There is no magical way to have such a tempered life. It must be achieved, by a process that toughens. This was true of the greatest Man who ever lived! "Although he was a Son, he learned obedience through what he suffered; and being made perfect . . ." (Heb. 5:8).

God gives you grace sufficient for every need through these trying days! He will, depend on that!

"My grace is sufficient for you . . ." (2 Cor. 12:9).

29 – Our Task

How'd you like to have a product everybody needed —with a world market . . . and no competition?

That is precisely true of the church of Christ!

She has had the Gospel committed to her . . .

It is indispensable to the eternal welfare of all men. . .

Its worldwide propagation is the mandate given to the church by her Lord.

No other institution has this message, this mandate or this market!

Think what a businessman would do in equivalent circumstances . . .

He'd make a killing!

But what of the church?

Again and again she has been guilty of downgrading the Gospel — marketing the same product, promoting the same program as all the other organizations.

Inevitably she loses her distinctiveness — becomes just one of many community organizations working for the "betterment of society."

No longer unique, she must compete with Community Chest, Red Cross, P.T.A., etc., for the energy, time, talent and money of men.

Inasmuch as churches seem to be offering the same service as other organizations, Mr. Citizen assumes he is doing his "Christian duty" without ever getting involved with the church.

And the churches have no one to blame but themselves.

Neglecting their unique task, propagation of the Gospel, they have defected to social, political and economic affairs, giving them priority.

Be absolutely sure of this: When churches default, service clubs, lodges, and community organizations are not going to proclaim the Gospel of Christ.

This is the consummate tragedy of modern Christendom: churches abandoning their calling to become just another community project involved with temporal affairs.

The apostle Paul has a word for us: "I decided to know nothing among you save Jesus Christ and him crucified. Woe to me if I do not preach the gospel" (1 Cor. 2:2; 9:16).

30 – Life Is a Gift

Assume eternal life were not the gift of God; that salvation were not "by grace through faith . . . ." Suppose salvation were of works. Suppose eternal life (whatever it means) had to be achieved rather than received. Would this not represent a terrible injustice on the part of God?

Think of those born of "bad blood," congenitally and constitutionally incapable of morality; having inherited weaknesses that make them pushovers to certain temptations they are unable to live a good enough life to "qualify" for heaven; or those reared in a tragic environment where they receive neither inclination or encouragement to "amount to anything" from either parents or neighbors. The climate in which they are reared is one in which evil and crime and immortality are normal and accepted; being good is difficult if not impossible with them.

47

On the other hand there are those born of good parents; reared in an ideal environment with every advantage; surrounded with respectability, guided carefully by parent and friends, educated to the "good life." Being good is almost "second nature" to them. If salvation were of works, to any degree whatever, millions would be predisposed to judgment without a ghost of a chance, victims of a birth and/or environment over which they had no control. What a diabolical unbalance this would be; what kind of a cruel god would invent such a system?

Eternal life is a gift to be received, not a goal to be achieved. Salvation is by the grace of God, through faith, by virtue of the sacrifice of the Son of God. Salvation is available to all men everywhere, whatever their condition, the circumstances of their birth or environment, inherited weaknesses or proneness to evil. In the economy of a God of perfect justice and love, salvation is given to any and all who will receive it.

Think it through. What other way of salvation could there be that would be non-exclusive and available to all irrespective of the "accidents" of birth and environment. The way of the cross is the one way.

"For God so loved the world that he gave his only Son, that whoever believes in him should not perish but have eternal life" (John 3:16).

31 — What Are You For?

It is not enough just to be against—or to be neutral. What are you for?

If you refuse the Christian way—what are your alternatives?

You will not believe in Christ . . .

In whom then will you believe?

You will not come to Christ . . .

To whom then will you go?

You will not follow Christ . . .

Whom then will you follow?

You believe something even if you insist that you don't believe in anything . . .

Believing in nothing is something!

You are following someone even if you insist you are following nobody.

You are living for something even if you're so busy making a living you do not know what you are living for.

You are going somewhere even if you have not bothered to get your direction or decide on your destination.

You are becoming someone even though you may be so completely preoccupied with the present that you ignore the future.

You've got a destiny—one way or the other—even though you are indifferent to it.

What are the alternatives if you will not have Christ —follow Christ—be Christ's—take Christ's way?

Honestly—do you know a better, more intelligent, more honorable and fulfilling way?

You're on your way . . . why not make it THE WAY? (John 14:6).

Jesus said, "He who is not with me is against me."

32 ~ God Is in Charge

The Christian says he believes God reigns . . . .

But often acts as though God had abdicated!

We profess to trust in God's overruling providence in the affairs of men and nations . . . but we live as though He had abandoned the world.

The Bible teaches by precept and example, thousands of precepts — thousands of examples, that God keeps in touch with His world and His people . . . that He is infinitely more interested than they in man's progress, individually and collectively.

God is not only interested in the process of history

. . . He is involved in it! And the outcome is completely in His control!

It is human impertinence to talk as though God were impersonal, aloof, and disinterested.

The apostle declared quite emphatically that in "everything God works for good with those who love him, who are called according to his purpose" (Rom. 8:28).

Why then do we ever give way to pessimism and despair?

In our saner moments, we know beyond the peradventure of a doubt that God is always the Master of all circumstances . . . never the victim of any! He is never taken by surprise . . . never thwarted . . . never frustrated. *God is in charge!*

Anxiety therefore is a kind of mistrust . . . a kind of challenge to God's integrity and fidelity.

Anxiety means that we believe in the circumstances more than we believe in God!

Things may look black at times . . . but *God is always bigger* than things.

The Christian is not an ostrich. He doesn't bury his head in the sand. He faces the facts, black, ugly, discouraging though they be . . . then He takes a long look at the *supreme fact*—the fact of Almighty God who is the Lord of the universe!

The Christian is realistic about circumstances . . . he is likewise realistic about God. The Christian is a realist all the way—not just half the way.

"The God who made the world and everything in it, being Lord of heaven and earth . . . gives to all men life and breath and everything . . . made from one every nation of men to live on all the face of the earth, having determined their allotted periods and the boundaries of their habitation" (Acts 17:24-26).

33 — Prayer Makes a Difference

Some things come only by prayer!

It is not accurate to say, "It will happen whether we pray or not." In many specifics, God waits to be asked.

Naturally there are many general blessings of God which come upon man without respect to the one who receives them. Rain falls upon the just and the unjust; the sun shines upon a man's fields whether he is good or wicked.

But in many of the specific blessings of life, the heavenly Father waits to be asked before He bestows them. Having made man a free moral agent, with a sovereign will of his own, God will not violate man's freedom by imposing upon him that which the man does not want. Therefore in many of the personal blessings of life, God gives as man requests.

And He will not give if man does not ask!

Prayer, rightly understood, is an integral part of man's relationship to God. By prayer man exposes himself to God's will, opens his heart to the wisdom of the heavenly Father, submits himself to the divine purpose. Prayer is not just getting things from God, though there is that aspect to it; it is consenting to God, yielding to God, once God's will has been made known through prayer.

Blessings falling upon a man whether he wants them or not, may turn out to be a curse. Getting accustomed to the good things, he is inclined to treat them with contempt; taking them for granted, he grows indifferent to the Giver.

"God's kindness is meant to lead you to repentance" (Rom. 2:4). Therefore blessings of God, received whether man asks for them or not, coming with commonplace regularity, may be the very thing which condemns a man. Indifferent to the Giver, he does not repent, and piles up judgment against himself.

In the economy of God the richest benefits of heaven are reserved for those who want them, who ask for them.

"You do not have, because you do not ask" (James 4:2). "Ask, and you will receive" (John 16:24, Jesus).

34 — The Gospel First

Do men really want peace?

Add up all the highest aspirations of men today—they are realized in the kingdom of God.

The kingdom of God means peace in the ultimate!

It means the elimination of racism — poverty — injustice—communication gaps—war—etc.

How do you explain this strange contradiction . . . ?

Men want what the kingdom of God offers. . . . but they do not want the kingdom of God?

They demand kingdom of God conditions—without kingdom of God requirements.

They want kingdom of God benefits—but they do not want to serve the King who makes those benefits possible.

They want God's blessings . . . *without God!*

Root of this dilemma is a simple human passion . . .

"I want my own way!"

Everybody wants a short cut to his dreams.

He wants his utopia the easy way . . .

Food without farming — wages without work — degrees without discipline — promotion without performance—values without value—peace without price.

Wanting one's own way is anarchy—order and anarchy are mutually exclusive—anarchy and chaos are synonymous.

Only God's order guarantees an ideal social environment—that is the kingdom of God.

Prerequisite to the kingdom is the Gospel without which there can be no kingdom.

If men want the kingdom, *they must accept the Gospel!*

"For in it the righteousness of God is revealed through faith for faith; as it is written, 'He who through faith is righteous shall live'" (Rom. 1:17).

35—Where Is the Cure for Degeneration?

"Without discipline, a human being becomes a barbarian no matter how much veneer is used to clothe the person in the trappings of the day." So declared the interesting and perceptive columnist, the late George E. Sokolsky, in his syndicated column, "These Days." The average reader will accept his statement without question. A man's experience with his own children or the neighbors', the memory of his childhood and the healthy correction of parental and/or educational discipline in his own life confirm the truth of Mr. Sokolsky's words.

Furthermore, Mr. Averageman is fully aware of the awful consequences of the lack of discpline, not only in children, but in adults as well. Most of us know firsthand the record of people or homes or businesses which were wrecked on the shoals of undisciplined lives. We know that without discipline a musician can never master his music; nor an artist his oils; nor a scholar his books; nor an executive his business; nor an athlete his sport. It is fundamental to our thinking that it takes discipline to beat par in golf, to rise above mediocrity in anything.

But the question is *Why?* What is the explanation for this thoroughly accepted fact that "without discipline a human being becomes a barbarian"? If human nature is the product of fortuitous circumstances set in motion by nothing several million (or billion, it is immaterial) years ago; if a man is nothing more than the refined result of spontaneous combustion a million or so generations removed, why should he degenerate so easily today? If collective man represents the inexorable advance through millenniums of indistinguishable ooze, why should individual man regress so easily!

Or is the Bible accurate when it speaks of man beginning from the hand of God as a perfect creation, which creation was marred by man's rebellion, which sin is reflected in the need for discipline if man is going to amount to anything? Universal experience verifies the wisdom of Jesus who insisted that man unaided by God could do nothing; that sin in the human heart was man's bottom problem, and that He Himself came to die on the cross as the divine solution to that problem, the only adequate cure for the disease of sin.

"What comes out of a man is what defiles a man" (Mark 7:20). "Apart from me you can do nothing" (John 15:5). "The blood of Jesus his Son cleanses us from all sin" (1 John 1:7).

36 — His Love Included Me

What is this love the Christian is supposed to emulate?

How big is it? Whom does it include?

How big is the love of God?

"God so loved the world . . ." (John 3:16).

Were unworthy men excluded from this love?

Were sinners excluded from this love?

Were rebels excluded from this love?

On the contrary, Paul insists that the supreme manifestation of this love is that ". . . while we were yet sinners, Christ died for us."

Did Christ's love include only those who accepted Him—exclude those who rejected Him?

If He did not exclude those who rejected Him—was His love wasted on them?

If the Christian's love is to measure up to God's standard, it must include those who are not Christian . . .

And it must include those who will never become Christian!

What kind of love is it that argues that love is to be given only where there is the possibility of evangelism happening?

What kind of ecclesiastical commercialism is it that will not show love where there is no possibility of the one being loved converting?

This is the sad caricature so often paraded by Christians as love today—the love that is reserved only for friends—only where there is some hope that conversion will follow.

Love that excludes anyone — whatever his response or indifference — is not the love of which the Bible speaks. It is phony. It is a denial of the love of God.

"Lord, when did we see thee hungry, and feed thee, or thirsty, and give thee drink? and when did we see thee a stranger and welcome thee, or naked and clothe thee? And when did we see thee sick or in prison and visit thee?" ". . . as you did it to one of the least of these my brethren, you did it to me" (Matt. 25:37-40).

37 — Prayer Is Not Weakness

"No atheists in fox holes . . . ." A familiar comment heard often during World War II.

Not always true perhaps, but the fact is that it was not uncommon for a tough fighting man to pray instinctively when under pressure; who, when the going was easy had disregarded or even ridiculed prayer. Many men testify to the surprise experienced when they found themselves praying in a tight spot, inasmuch as they had always figured that prayer was "for the birds."

Nothing abnormal about this: Man was made for

fellowship with God. His spirit demands the atmosphere of heaven just as his body needs oxygen on earth. True, a man may neglect his relationship with the heavenly Father and seem to be getting along nicely, but actually his soul is drying up within him. And the real tragedy is that he may not be aware of this spiritual death until it is too late!

The strongest man who ever lived needed to pray constantly!

The wisest man who ever lived claimed that prayer was absolutely essential to life.

He never made a decision without first praying. Every crisis in His life was faced by prayer. Often He was to be found alone in prayer—long before the sun broke over the horizon to begin a new day. It was not unusual for Him to spend all night in prayer. His life is the standard, the norm, the perfect example of what man ought to be, and prayer was at the heart of His life.

If Jesus Christ needed to pray, how much more ought we to pray! Pray daily, pray often, pray regularly. Don't worry about "how" to pray, just pray. Seek God's face, ask Christ to help you, to teach you to pray.

"[Men] ought always to pray and not lose heart" (Jesus Christ in Luke 18:1).

38 — But You Can

"I can't!"

The most elementary form of self-justification.

"I can't!"

Therefore, I don't have to!

Hence a child—in his own little mind and in his own little way explains his failure . . . or his refusal.

It may be excusable in a child . . . it is unpardonable in an adult!

Nevertheless, many of us, grown to manhood, justify our failure and our abdication.

And settle for mediocrity!

Like pouting adolescents, we refuse to stop a bad habit or do a good deed . . . and justify it by saying, "I can't!"

The simple fact is—*a man can do anything he really wants to do*—if he submits his will to God!

When a man really wants to break a bad habit . . . or be adequate for a difficult task . . .

God will enable him!

In other words—a man fails . . . not because he can't live up to his resolution or profession — but *because he doesn't want to.*

He says he does . . . but the subterfuge is, "I can't!"

Jesus was a perfect man. He said those who believe in Him could "do the works that I do . . ."

Because the Holy Spirit would be given to those who believed in Him — the same One who enabled Jesus to do what He did.

"Apart from me you can do nothing," Jesus said. That's fact number one in the walk of faith . . .

"I can do all things in him who strengthens me!" That's the corollary . . . and it works!

39 — Ultimate Love

You can't make God stop loving you!

You may ignore Him, resist Him, insult Him, reject Him. You may commit every sin "in the book," do every damnable thing that was ever conceived as sin; but you can't make God stop loving you!

God loves man because it is the nature of God to love. God loves, not because man is lovable; not because man deserves to be loved; but because God is love. God is not fickle nor capricious. He is unchangeable, and therefore He never stops loving, no matter how unworthy a man may be of His love. God's love is the opposite of man's love: human love is stimulated by the beloved, depends upon the "lovability" of the one loved. Human love is not capable of loving that which is unlovely or unlovable. Man loves because there is something in the beloved that inspires that love. Therefore man loves, or stops loving, depending upon his relationship with another.

The love of God depends upon the lover. Whether or not the beloved inspires love, God loves him. God's love is irrespective of the beloved. God's love is irrevocable, unchangeable, eternal, inexhaustible.

You can't make God stop loving you, but you can be indifferent to His love, you can refuse His love, reject it entirely. Love does not force or coerce. Love respects the rights of the beloved, and God's love is no exception. He will not force His intentions. He has made known His love for you supremely in the cross of His Son. (If you are ever tempted to doubt God's love for you, remember the cross!)

But no man has to believe in the cross. No man has to accept it. You can ignore it, reject it. This, in fact, is the greatest sin a man can commit. It is the unpardonable sin. To reject God's love in Jesus Christ is to reject God's provision for man's redemption from sin and its present and eternal consequences. Every sin of man is covered by the cross, except the sin of rejection.

"God shows his love for us in that while we were yet sinners Christ died for us" (Rom. 5:8).

40 — Christian, Be Yourself!

In a real sense Christian witness is a secret service.

The Christian who takes seriously his duty to God and man — who desires to exert a positive and constructive influence for Christ where he lives — has no infallible criteria whereby he may know how he is doing.

In fact, those most deeply influenced by him may not be aware of that influence in the process.

As the sun can tan a body without the conscious awareness of the one being tanned, so the Godly influence of a thoughtful Christian may sink in and affect other lives without their knowledge.

And the serious Christian is not aware of the transmission of his influence. He is just being himself—committed to Christ—dependent upon the Holy Spirit.

Today, in a hundred million places around the world Christ-possessed, Christ-filled persons will go quietly to their tasks and places in society and throughout the day they will be permeating that society like a "benevolent infection" with Christian influence.

They will not advertise — will not sound a trumpet before them — may not even talk a lot about it.

They will not preach—will not "evangelize" in the conventional sense . . . but they will be a sermon—their lives will "witness" to the reality and relevance of Christ.

Today, parliaments, offices, schools and campuses, labor unions, military installations, clubs, markets, homes all over the world, will be silently infiltrated by faithful Christians whose lives, managed by the Holy Spirit, will bless and sweeten and challenge and preserve the little world in which they move.

This is the heart and soul of the impact of the church in the world. This is the cutting edge — the point of thrust—the center of impact of authentic Christian witness and influence as it penetrates the secular system.

Jesus said, "You are the salt of the earth." Salt is useless as long as it retains its identity in the salt shaker . . .

Only as it is spread on the food—losing its identity as it disappears—does it enhance and make palatable and preserve.

So faithful Christians—"rubbed" by Christ into the society around them — disappear as they dissolve into that secular structure . . .

And there, daily, they enhance and make palatable and preserve . . . and make men thirsty for God and righteousness.

Congratulations—Salt of the earth!

41 — The Ministry of the Layman

The apostolic church was a lay movement. Jesus did not choose His disciples from youth still unsettled and uncertain of their future; He chose men for whom life had jelled, hardened men, veterans of a vocation in which they had won their spurs. These businessmen and laboring men were His witnesses!

On the day of Pentecost 120 disciples gathered in the Upper Room. Whatever happened that day happened to every one of them. They were not "professionals," clergymen with theological degrees; they were "run-of-the-mill" people like you meet daily everywhere. But they all witnessed and 3,000 devout Jews heard them and were baptized as Christians. These Jews were laymen, from every nation, who undoubtedly returned to their homelands and witnessed for Christ.

Subsequently heavy persecution forced all Christians out of Jerusalem (except the apostles), and wherever they were scattered they "went preaching the gospel." It was the laymen who were scattered!

The first martyr, Stephen, was a layman.

The first evangelist, Philip, was a layman.

For that matter, Paul himself, the first missionary, never did discontinue his vocation of tent making.

A man will never understand the church of Jesus Christ until he sees it as a lay movement, not an organization top heavy with clergy and dominated by "professionals." As a matter of fact the work of the ministry belongs to the laymen. In Ephesians 4:11, 12, the apostle Paul states that some were apostles, some were prophets, some evangelists, some pastors and teachers, that they might train all Christians "to do the work of the ministry." This is the divine pattern, and the task of the church depends upon the active participation of every member.

God has placed you where you are that you may be His contact there. The preacher, the evangelist cannot reach where they are not; you're there, where you are, as God's connection with those around you. The preaching of the Word, verified by the witness of the Christian, has a double-barreled impact that penetrates paganism and secularism. Preaching alone, without the witness, fails of the mark.

The man who knows Christ has something to say; the man who has nothing to say probably does not know Christ. Whatever else a Christian does, this one thing is required of him, that he be a witness to the relevancy of Jesus Christ and the Gospel.

". . . You shall receive power when the Holy Spirit has come upon you; and you shall be my witnesses" (Acts 1:8).

42 — A Wrong Appetite

Spiritual lust!

It often passes for piety . . .

But it leads to disillusionment and despair.

It never pays off—never satisfies—never fulfills.

Jesus said that those who believed in Him would never thirst again.

Thirst comes when the Christian seeks his satisfaction in something else than Jesus.

In the name of spirituality there are those who seek added "blessing . . ."

Demanding something more—preoccupied with the gifts rather than the Giver.

61

It's like drinking salt water—more you have, thirstier you get.

Thirst increases with every effort to assuage it.

That leads to the jaded life—the spent life—the satiated but unsatisfied life—the dried out, wrinkled, barren life.

Anything more than Jesus for satisfaction always turns out to be less than Jesus!

When Jesus Himself is your satisfaction, you never thirst again.

He is always more than enough for any man!

He is everything man needs — and everything God gives.

It will require forever for the whole human family — the entire cosmos — to understand His infinite, incomprehensible love and grace.

Jesus said to them, "I am the bread of life; he who comes to me shall not hunger, and he who believes in me shall never thirst . . . I am the living bread which came down from heaven; if any one eats of this bread, he will live forever . . ." (John 6:35, 51).

Paul said, "In him the whole fulness of deity dwells bodily, and you have come to fulness of life in him" (Col. 2:9, 10).

43 — Only Man's Best Is Good Enough

The good golfer never plays against his opponent; he plays against par. A good runner runs against time; a good bowler works for 300. Few records would be set on the golf course, on the track, in the bowling alley, if men simply played to beat their opponents. Tendency would be just to keep ahead of the other fellow; satisfaction would rest in that, rather than in beating records. When they play against par, time, a perfect 300, the golfer shoots his best game; the runner runs his best race, etc. The goal demands top performance, not just enough to beat somebody else. On the other hand, a mediocre game may be sufficient to beat an opponent, still your game stops far short of the top.

In other words the man who aims at little will probably hit it!

This works in other places too: business, factory, shop. Try just to be better than the other fellow; you may achieve that and still do half the job. The world is full of men just a little bit better than someone else. History is made by men who shoot for par! Fortunes have been made by men who do more than just try to beat out competition, whether it is making the best hamburger, pie, ice cream, or the best car. Whether it is running a machine or an office. Men who go all-out for the best make the world.

Skid row is spotted with men who never did more than they were paid for, who worked just hard enough to "get by," who thought it was smart when they could "put one over" on the boss. That is another way of saying failure, just doing what I am paid to do, nothing more. Wages are paid to the man who does just what he is paid to do. Salaries are paid to those who do whatever needs to be done when it needs to be done, and do their best!

The Christian man ought never be satisfied with less than his best in his job. His goal is the glory of God. He does his work realizing that God is interested in what he produces, and how he does it. Whether it is working in an assembly line or a plush office, the Christian does his outside best, not because he is paid for it, but because only his best is enough. The world needs men like that, men who are not simply trying to be better than somebody else, but who are striving to be God's best.

God's glory is "par" for the Christian. "Whether you eat or drink, or whatever you do, do all to the glory of God" (1 Cor. 10:13).

44 — The Worth of a Man

There's something worse than contempt for property!
Contempt for persons!
As far as Jesus is concerned
    you cannot pile enough property together
        to equal the value of one man . . .
Any man!
Jesus didn't love property.
He loved people
           . . . and used property.
We tend to use people
            . . . and love property.
Jesus did not die for property.
He died for people!
Property has its place in the Christian view of life.
    It is to be treated as a trust from God.
    It requires careful stewardship.
    It is to be used to the glory of God . . .
And the benefit of persons!
Handled any other way
           it becomes

                    a curse!

The value of one man
           any man . . .
Is incalculable.
All the wealth of the world does not add up to the
worth of one man!
"What shall it profit a man if he gain the whole
world and lose his own soul? What will a man give in
exchange for his soul?" — Jesus.

45 — Man's Plight — God's Remedy

How do you explain the fact that if you let a thing
go it deteriorates, degenerates? Whether machinery or

men, leave them alone and they break down, clog up, wear out, go to pieces.

Life demands constant care and unrelenting watchfulness. Why?

Why, for example, is "eternal vigilance the price of freedom"? How come freedom isn't automatic? Why isn't freedom the natural thing that comes easily? Why should we have to fight a war for it every few years, then be forced to guard it with unwavering, unremitting care in times of peace? Grow careless and anarchy, or tyranny, take over.

If evolutionists are accurate in their theories that the world has evolved from nothing to something, from the simple to the complex, from ooze to man; if progress is built in, how come man's history has been scarred from the beginning by this strange retrogression?

To be sure a child grows to manhood properly equipped for life is a matter of continual, constant supervision and instruction; and once he is a man, he must practice self-discipline. Collective man makes giant advances in technology and science, and this progress constitutes a threat to his survival. Man in and of himself doesn't make a very optimistic picture! Does the roof have to fall in on us before we learn from history?

Jesus insisted that there was a malignancy in the heart of man which was the root of his trouble (Mark 7:14ff). For this reason He entered history. He gave His life on a cross for the redemption of mankind and no solution short of Jesus' sacrifice is adequate! Man is doomed to futility, individually and collectively, unless and until he recognizes in Jesus Christ God's answer for man's dilemma.

"I am not ashamed of the gospel: it is the power of God for salvation to every one who has faith" (Rom. 1:16).

46 ~ Two Kinds of Men

You have often heard human nature referred to as a stream — the "stream of humanity." Have you ever considered how really like a stream it is?

As the stream has its source in the highlands—the virgin, snow-clad peaks—so human nature had its beginning with God. Man was the peak of God's perfected creation. After everything else He made man—in His own image—for fellowship with Himself.

But the stream leaves its source—so man has turned from God . . . left God out of his life—lived as though God didn't matter.

Down hill flows the stream—seeking irresistibly the lowest levels . . . never stopping—over and around—under and across—restlessly—impatiently—sometimes laughingly . . . it flows—lower and lower.

Human nature too seeks its lowest level . . . down —down—down to moral decay and spiritual ruin . . . But some will point to the progress—the advancement humanity has made. True! But only along technological lines . . . not morally or spiritually!

As the stream moves down the incline, it is constantly picking up dirt—debris—spoilage—carrying it along—adding to its corruption . . . except

Here and there in its path are rocks. They will not move with the stream—will not loosen and float down-hill—will not yield to the irresistible descent! These rocks purify the stream every few rods.

There are rocks in human nature! Men who refuse to budge—immovable! Christian men—solid—clean—courageous. They will not yield to the descent — will not compromise. These men purify the life about them in the home—the office—the plant—in society.

Two kinds of men! Those who yield to the pull downward—who gravitate to the lower levels . . . and become part of the corrupting influence. Those who refuse to yield—who stand against the tide—who keep humanity from rotting altogether! To which group of men do you belong?

Finally the stream finds its way to the ocean—dumps into it—is lost in its abysmal depths . . . unless—and until—the sun lifts it back again into the heavenlies.

Human nature too ends in the abyss . . . unless—it allows itself to be lifted by the Son of God—who laid down His life on the cross to redeem it. When a man yields to the pull of the Son, he is lifted back into fellowship with God!

One of the great historians of our day says the history of civilization can be told in one phrase of the New Testament: "The wages of sin is death . . ."

"The wages of sin *is* death, but the free gift of God is eternal life . . ." (Rom. 6:23).

47 — Christian Character

What constitutes character anyway? What is the difference between a good man and a bad man? We've got our wires crossed a lot here!

Some say a man's creed is the final test for Christian character. What a man believes is the thing! This is important—a man can't be a Christian if he believes wrongly about God and Christ. Christian character begins with right belief—but it doesn't end there. There are plenty who have a good creed—and live like the devil. The Bible says that "the devils believe — and tremble." That's as far as it goes! There's more to character than just what a man believes.

Others say a man's conduct is the test for Christian character. Watch how a man acts—what he does—and you can determine whether or not he is a Christian. Not necessarily . . . . You can be wrong on a man's conduct. He can order his conduct to achieve very selfish ends. He may do nice things — to accomplish bad purposes. Some men treat you well—just to get a business advantage. Buy you lunch—so they can sell you something! His conduct is not prompted by interest in you—he's interested only in what he can get out of you.

Just like a lot of business deals—same principle—bigger stakes!

Anyway—it's not a new thing: fellow acting like a good man until the stage is set to steal—or kill—or exploit. We call it "Fifth Column." Wouldn't be so serious if this weren't so normal today! Great deal of business is run just like that. Buy a man a drink—take him to lunch—play golf with him—buy him a gift—why? For his sake? *No!* For your sake. You want something from him—or he wants something from you.

Real test for Christian character is not creed or conduct or a lot of other things men judge by. Real test is a man's motives. Not what he does—but why he does it! Man's motive is the thing you must fear most in them. You can never trust a man with false motives—no matter how well he behaves. God is more concerned about your motives than anything else in your life. The tragedy is that men are busy making a living—and they don't know what they're living for. Examine your motives daily—then guard them.

"For the Lord sees not as man sees; man looks on the outward appearance, but the Lord looks on the heart" (1 Sam. 16:7).

48 — Faith Comes By . . .

Faith does not come by struggle!

Faith is effortless . . .

The quiet response of a man's heart to one who is trustworthy.

It's deeper than an intellectual response.

In fact—it is not uncommon to trust someone you do not completely understand.

Jesus' disciples often did not understand Him . . .
But they trusted Him!
His words at times were incomprehensible . . .
Nevertheless He inspired confidence.
Except in those who would not accept Him.
Not that they could not . . . they would not!
Thomas had some doubts on occasion . . .
Jesus satisfied them so thoroughly that he could declare, "My Lord and my God."

The man who says he cannot believe in Jesus Christ should examine himself—ask himself if he is willing to believe.

If he is willing but cannot—Jesus will meet him in some faith-generating way that will resolve his difficulty.

If he is unwilling—there is nothing Jesus—or anyone else can do to convince him.

(No man is convinced against his will.)

Obviously evidence is meaningless to the man who refuses it.

"Faith comes from what is heard and what is heard comes by the preaching of Christ" (Rom. 10:17).

49 — Truth and Error

God's mind is made up in spiritual matters . . . as surely as it is in moral or physical matters. There are laws of the spirit as there are moral and physical laws. There is right and wrong in spiritual life—as there is right and wrong in moral life and physical life. Take life seriously—and any other idea is unthinkable—abhorrent—untenable! This is an orderly universe. It is a cosmos—not chaos physically. It is a cosmos—not chaos morally. And it is a cosmos spiritually! Anarchy is just as wrong—just as diabolical—just as destructive spiritually as it is other ways.

Certainly there is truth in religion! And if truth, there is falsehood! Yet men allow themselves to be misled into sheer anarchy in the field of religion as though right and wrong were not important here. Under the guise of tolerance they accept anything! As the moral is above the physical so the spiritual is above the moral. In this highest realm, the realm of the spirit, the right way is more important—more basic—than in any other realm. One need not be misled in spiritual things. There is a right and a way to know it! There is a wrong and a way to know that too! There are two solid criteria, two facts by which we may test for truth . . .

First is the Gospel—a simple statement of the fact that God Himself did something at a certain time in history. God intervened in human affairs. His intervention was to save man from his headlong plunge to self-destruction. God came to restore man to his rightful place . . . fellowship with God. The Gospel declares that man's condition is hopeless and helpless. That he is lost and being lost can do nothing to remedy his lostness. It tells of a God who is seeking man — to save him—to give him eternal life. This Gospel is the antithesis of all false religions which, in one way or another, declare man to be capable of saving himself . . . whether by ethics or idealogy—or simply learning to think right. ". . . all have sinned and fall short of the glory of God, they are justified by his grace as a gift, through the redemption which is in Christ Jesus" (Rom. 3:23, 24). "For I delivered unto you as of first importance [the Gospel] . . . that Christ died for our sins in accordance with the scriptures, that he was buried, that he was raised on the third day in accordance with the scriptures . . ." (1 Cor. 15:3, 4).

Second test for truth is the Incarnation! By this is meant that in the Person of Jesus Christ, God Himself became a man in order to reconcile man to Himself. All there is of God was in that historical figure who bore the name of Jesus Christ. A man's religion rises or falls in terms of this fact: "God was in Christ!"

"Who is the liar but he who denies that Jesus is the

Christ? (1 John 2:22). "Every spirit which confesses that Jesus Christ has come in the flesh is of God, and every spirit which does not confess Jesus is not of God" (1 John 4:2, 3).

50 — In His Name

Is Jesus Christ an embarrassment to you?

It is understandable when disciples of non-Christian religions find the name of Jesus Christ offensive. But what a contradiction when those who profess to be Jesus' disciples are embarrassed by His name.

As a matter of fact, not uncommonly in a public meeting, it is the "Christian" more than the non-Christian who cringes when Jesus Christ is spoken of reverently.

On one occasion I was invited to pray at a convention luncheon. The chairman, a Protestant minister, informed me that forty percent of those present were Jewish and requested that I delete the name of Jesus Christ from my prayer.

"Suppose a Jewish Rabbi were praying," I asked the chairman, "would you request that he close his prayer in the name of Jesus Christ inasmuch as the majority of those present were probably Catholic and Protestant?"

"But that's different!" he replied. (He didn't explain.)

As a Christian does not expect a Jewish Rabbi to pray in the name of Jesus Christ, a Jew expects a Christian minister to pray in the name of Jesus Christ. It certainly does no honor to Jewish friends to compromise here.

The world will not be surprised when Christians honor their Savior and Lord . . . if anything, they wonder why disciples of Christ often seem so defensive and apologetic about Him.

Jesus Christ in all His beauty and power—His perfection and timelessness is that which gives the church its uniqueness and relevance.

Apart from Him the church is just another community organization distinguished only by its ecclesiastical accoutrements but with no more relevance (if anything less) than a service club or the P.T.A.

There is blessing and power in the name of Jesus Christ when spoken with faith and conviction . . .

He incarnates peace and love—healing and reconciliation.

"Therefore God has highly exalted him and bestowed on him the name which is above every name, that at the name of Jesus every knee should bow, in heaven, and on earth, and under the earth . . ." (Phil. 2:9, 10).

51 — Little Man — Big Bluff

The following story is told by the late Bennett Cerf in his book, *Good for a Laugh* published by Bantam Books, New York.

"The president of a great southern railroad is noted for his patience and humility. He says he got a lesson he never forgot the first day he was appointed station master in a tiny Mississippi way-stop.

"Two Negro farmers came along to ask some questions regarding a bill of lading, and the new official decided to put on the dog. The Negroes waited patiently while he bustled about the station doing nothing . . . .

"Finally one said very distinctly to the other, 'Dat's life for you, brother! De littler de station—de bigger de agent.' What the young official learned that moment helped make him president of the road."

Why is it some men can't seem to realize how transparent their pretentions are? Their efforts to impress only expose their littleness!

Visiting in a home where there were two dogs made the railroad story more meaningful. One dog was a tiny Mexican Chihuahua not more than six inches high, but what a noise he made. He challenged our right to enter, then followed us around nipping at our heels, barking and snapping and fussing. (He did not frighten us!) The other dog was a Great Dane. He barely lifted his head when we entered, turned it slightly to look at us, then with huge head on paws watched us walk down the hall. Later we returned to find the Chihuahua challenging the Great Dane. With much barking and activity he flashed back and forth over and around the big dog who meanwhile patiently endured the antics.

Men come like that too: The little fellow who always has to prove something. Always proclaiming his rights. He is usually loud and boastful and cocky. He drives his car as though he owned the boulevard, dares anyone to "make something of it." Chip on shoulder he is always challenging someone. (This has nothing to do with size. Some of the most courageous men have been small of stature. It has to do with inner resources!) He demands the center of the stage as he continually works at impressing others. Actually he is just a bother; nobody takes him seriously.

What the little man does not see is that his strutting actually testifies to his own inner weakness, fear or inadequacy. What he really impresses men with is his unimportance. If a man has something, he does not have to prove it. If he does not, talking will do no good. Humility is a sign of greatness. Conceit inevitably confirms emptiness and failure. The big man is humble, quiet, gentle.

"For everyone who exalts himself will be humbled, and he who humbles himself will be exalted" (Luke 14:11).

52 – Confusion!

Our characteristic syndrome in the Seventies.

One reason is our failure (or unwillingness) to recognize behind all the outward alienation and conflict a spiritual warfare whose chief protagonist is a spiritual being—the incarnation of evil.

Every conflict of history is that basic conflict surfacing within and midst humanity. Contemporary conflicts: Vietnam, racial, industrial, domestic, and personal, are symptoms of this profound war between Satan and Christ.

It is a maxim of life that *one must know who his enemy is* before he is able to oppose him effectively.

Our chief enemy generates enmity among us so that we fight among ourselves—make enemies where there are none:—Americans vs. Japanese—whites vs. blacks—management vs. labor—husband vs. wife and parent vs. child.

For that matter, our enemy can be anyone who accidentally cuts in on us in traffic.

This is the supreme strategy of the one adversary of man. He is the master of incognito. He uses any device which will pit man against man.

And all the while he convinces man of his own non-existence.

He uses our intellects against us. Who's afraid of what isn't?

Satan pursues his evil program in history—by whatever means to defeat Jesus Christ and His kingdom—by whatever means to lure man into final allegiance to himself.

He divides to conquer: promoting disorder—disunity—alienation—anarchy—rebellion . . .

And we'll continue to be victimized until we see that the basic problem is not economic or social or political or military or psychological . . .

The basic problem is spiritual!

The deepest issue in history is theological.

If we will not submit to the rule of God we sentence ourselves to perpetual tyranny. If we will not conform to the order of God we invite increasing disorder.

"We are not contending against flesh and blood, but against the principalities, against the powers, against the world rulers of this present darkness" (Eph. 6:12).

53 — Absolute Perfection — No Less!

How could God settle for anything less than perfection?

How could He, who is eternally aflame with moral perfection, countenance a man who had morally failed? If God be God, then perfection is normal; the condition which must be met before fellowship with Him is possible. The idea of man coming to God on man's terms is ridiculous on the surface. Let any man think it over; he must realize that an approach to God could be made only on God's terms; and perfection is the only possible condition whereby God could receive man.

Hence Jesus, in the Sermon on the Mount, said, "You must be perfect as your heavenly Father is perfect." Anything less than perfection will never make it. An imperfect man, morally corrupt, would be destroyed the moment he came into contact with the blazing holiness of God.

Does this mean then that man's approach to God is impossible? For man yes; but with God nothing is impossible. Man cannot make himself perfect; but God has made a way whereby a man can actually enjoy the perfection of God.

This is the incredible truth of the Gospel.

God has provided a way that His perfection can be imputed, and imparted to imperfect man, and man, who has morally failed, can have rapport with God without fear of judgment or destruction. Jesus never intended that the Sermon on the Mount, or the Golden Rule, or any other ethical or moral code for that matter, were to be the means whereby man might achieve by his own effort rightness with God.

(Nothing is more thoroughly documented in history than man's incapacity to keep the law of God, a fact which does not surprise God.)

The perfect law of God, whether expressed in the Sermon on the Mount or the Ten Commandments, was given as a standard by which man could be made aware of his failure and sin; and realizing the futility of his own effort to lift himself up by his own bootstraps, might turn to God for the help offered in Jesus Christ's Gospel. In the Gospel God lays down the requirement for salvation, and the provision by which this requirement is met in His Son.

Eternal life is not a goal to be achieved; it is a gift to be received.

"I am not ashamed of the gospel: it is the power of God for salvation to every one who has faith . . . For in it [Gospel] the righteousness of God is revealed through faith for faith; as it is written, 'He who through faith is righteous shall live' " (Rom. 1:16, 17).

54 — A Member of the Family

My personal relationship to Jesus Christ is fundamental to Christian faith . . .

In fact, it is of the essence of Christian faith.

To practice the ethics is not enough . . .

To profess the doctrine is not enough . . .

To perform the liturgy is not enough.

No man is a Christian in the New Testament sense who is not related to Jesus Christ by personal acceptance of Him—His love and grace.

This is the essentially individual, personal, private aspect of faith.

Christ cannot be inherited—He must be personally received.

But neither is a man Christian in the New Testament sense who is not rightly related to others . . .

Because the moment a man receives Christ, he becomes part of the family; he is irresistibly joined to an indivisible, inseparable fellowship.

Reconciliation is at the heart of Christian faith . . .

Reconciliation of man with God and man to man.

Having been reconciled to God in Christ, the true Christian seeks reconciliation with his brothers in Christ . . .

And he seeks the reconciliation of others to God and to those who are brothers in Christ.

He has been given the message and the ministry of reconciliation — constrained by the love of Christ, he becomes an ambassador for Christ.

This compulsion to reconciliation is native to the true Christian . . . its absence betrays some disconnection between the Christian and the Spirit of God who motivates always to reconciliation.

Love for God is an illusion if it is not accompanied by love for man.

The two great commandments are really one.

". . . he who does not love his brother whom he has seen, cannot love God whom he has not seen" (1 John 4:20).

55 ~ The Ministry of Listening

Are your conversations about Christ dialogue, or duel?

We are so prone to talk *at* people. Jesus talked *with* them! Our conversations are so often monologues; Jesus' were always dialogues.

Jesus listened, really touched man's need. We listen badly because while the other man is talking, we're preoccupied with what we're going to say next. Instead of helping him understand, we pursue our stereotyped argument; and as soon as he's through talking (or before), we jab and spar with clichés which probably mean nothing to him. We keep busy delivering little sermonettes in between his remarks.

Soon he gets the feeling this is an "I—You" relationship rather than "We." He's on the outside; we're on the inside and he's unwelcome unless he is able to pass rather rigid specifications; about which he won't bother because he's lost interest in being an "insider"; life seems more friendly and warm on the outside of our pat little stereotyped world. We may have won the argument, but we lost the man, alienated him with our "air-right" case when we should have warmed him with Christ's love. Jesus' gentle invitation, "Come unto me . . ." we harden into a cold, inflexible obstruction. The Door we bar with language, the Way we make a wall.

There is only one Gospel! It is God's eternal answer to man's perennial sin. It is as valid, as relevant to man's need today as it was when the Son of God shed His blood on the cross, was buried, rose again nineteen centuries ago. That Gospel is more than words; it was love in action; love on a cross: thorn-crowned brow, nail-pierced hands and feet, a broken heart. Such a Gospel is not commended with anger and argument. It is the Word become loving, compassionate flesh!

If your vocal witness is a monologue; modern, sophisticated man, inoculated with religion, will turn down his "hearing aid" and politely wait to escape from such a one-sided engagement.

Wrote the apostle Paul: "The Lord's servant must not be quarrelsome but be kindly to all men . . . Our gospel came to you not only in word . . . We were gentle among you, like a nurse taking care of her children . . . we were ready to share with you not only the gospel of God, but also our own selves."

56 — The Real Hero

The real hero is not the man who sets out to be one.

The real hero is the man who interprets the issues correctly and responds to the need intelligently.

He does what has to be done!

Some men with a hero's complex and compulsion invent issues—or attack them before they are ripe.

In the interests of being a hero they actually confuse the issues and compound the problems.

And their solutions are always premature . . .

Because the real motive behind such abortive action is not the solution of the problem but the passion to be a hero.

Tragically, such compulsive heroes lead their followers to impasse, disillusion and frustration.

They complicate matters and postpone settlements.

The first prerequisite for authentic heroism is selflessness!

Nothing is further from a true hero's mind than being a hero.

It is foreign to his thinking. He is surprised when treated like a hero—embarrassed by the publicity—unwilling to accept the adulation.

As far as he is concerned, he did what had to be done . . .

He saw a need and without thought for self plunged in to do what he could.

With cosmic problems erupting as they are today, men need to think soberly and selflessly before they act!

Too many little men see a chance to be heroes— and they are raising issues artificially and stirring up reaction that only aggravates the problem.

"He who believes will not be in haste" (Isa. 28:16).

"It is required of stewards that they be found faithful" (1 Cor. 4:2).

57 — Responsibility in Leadership

The larger the rock you drop in a quiet pool the greater the ripples that radiate out from the splash washing across everything in their way as they circle toward the edge of the water. This is obvious when it comes to dropping pebbles in puddles, but what is equally obvious, yet too often overlooked by men, is the same identical principle in life! A man's impact moves out from him in concentric waves touching everyone within the sphere of his influence with greater or less force, depending on the man!

The bigger the man, the greater his impact! Good or bad, it influences those around him. His sin moves out to cover the crowd, just as much as his righteousness. The little man can get away with things a big man ought never do. Because the little man is not noticed like the big man. His actions and attitudes do not register with the same force.

The fact that a man has risen to a place of power and prestige doubles or triples or quadruples his responsibility. His life is continually influencing others, consciously or unconsciously. The greater the heights he has reached, the more important his position, the more eagerly people follow him. He becomes an example: the standard, the norm, right or wrong, by virtue of his position. His life becomes a goal toward which other men strive.

Either they deliberately copy the big man, thinking they are finding his secret of success, or else the fact that he does a thing, or does not, means approval or disapproval to them. If the big man does it, it's O.K.! In either case it is dangerous because often men who imitate actually imitate the superficial, the secondary, the idiosyncrasy, or the thing that is safe for the big man may destroy those who follow him.

Whether a man likes it or not, if he is in a place

of leadership, he will be influencing others. He has no right just to consider himself. He must think in terms of his influence. This is part of the price of leadership! Not just the man himself, but what happens to those who follow in his footsteps, is the serious responsibility of the leader, the big man! This is inescapable!

"To whom much is given, of him will much be required!" (Jesus, Luke 12:48).

58 — Being in the Right Place

One of the most difficult temptations to resist at any time, but especially in these crucial, explosive days, is the temptation that I ought to be some place else doing something other than I'm doing.

This is the stubborn and subtle intimidation insinuated by the "where-the-action-is" philosophy.

Of course it does not concern the apathetic or indifferent whose number is legion.

Nor does it bother those who are of "the cult of the status quo"—they just worry.

But it frustrates good men who take seriously the festering circumstances of our times.

They are moved by tragedy and need . . .

They are disturbed by violence and war and their threatening escalation.

They are troubled by reaction which in itself is a serious threat to justice, freedom and order.

Their concern causes them to challenge their own status quo . . .

Are they where they ought to be—doing what they ought to be doing?

Are they part of the solution or do they just compound the problem?

Are they just observers—mere spectators—looking on while the world explodes?

These are the questions that burn in their hearts!

Resolution comes when one gives himself to Christ —asks, "Christ, what will You have me to do?"

If one is not where he belongs, Christ will lead him where he ought to be. If he is not doing what he ought to do, Christ will show him the appointed task.

Try it! Paul did . . . and it worked for him!

59 — Assurance Is Not Pride

A tract tells the story of an "inquiring photographer" on the *New York Daily News* who asked the following question of six persons: "What are your chances of going to heaven when you die?" The answers that he received indicated an almost complete ignorance of the teaching of the Bible concerning the subject.

One said that she personally had no chance, but that her father, now dead, had been a fine man, and would probably put in a "good word" for her. The second ridiculed the idea with the comment that since he had not learned to play the harp his chances were probably slim. Another felt that his wife's chances were fair because she had joined the church of her choice. The rest gave answers which expressed in one way or another the idea that getting to heaven depended on a man's achievements. Every answer revealed uncertainty about heaven as though, if there were such a place, one could not be sure of going there when he died.

This is in direct disagreement with the whole tone and temper of the Bible. For the Bible expressly teaches that it is possible for a man to know now, before he dies, that heaven is assured. In fact the Bible urges this assurance on a man. There are, of course, those who feel that it is unmitigated conceit for a person to say he knows that he has eternal life. But such an idea confirms a lack of knowledge of the Scriptures.

For a man to be sure of heaven does not mean that he is taking credit to himself. It does not mean that he holds any sense of superiority. On the contrary, it means that he has acknowledged his sin, has received Christ as his Savior; and is trusting not himself but Jesus Christ! Because no man can earn his salvation. No man can live good enough, pile up good deeds enough, to achieve heaven. The man who gets to heaven makes it, wholly and solely, on the grounds of the sacrifice of Christ!

Actually for a believer to question his salvation, is for him to doubt the ability of Jesus Christ to save; is for him to doubt the grace of God. Declared the apostle John: "I write this to you who believe in the name of the Son of God, that you may know that you have eternal life" (1 John 5:13). John wrote to give assurance to the believer in Jesus Christ. Paul states: ". . . I know whom I have believed, and I am sure that he is able to guard until that day what has been entrusted to me" (2 Tim. 1:12). Paul did not hope, nor wish, nor guess; he knew for sure! He was persuaded!

". . . God gave us eternal life, and this life is in his Son. He who has the Son has life" (1 John 5:11, 12). You too may know; if you receive Christ, trust Him.

60 — Kingdom of God Men

You can't have kingdom of God society without kingdom of God men!

Which fact is at the heart of the world's frustration today.

Education hasn't been able to manage it . . .

Legislation hasn't been able to manage it . . .

No political, economic or social organization has been able to manage it!

Over and over man experiments with the same old systems.

One fails—he tries another which in turn fails until he has used up all his options and then rebounds to the first system again with whatever refinements increased knowledge affords.

And with all his present knowledge — with all the compounded experience of former generations—with all the lessons of history . . .

Man goes on making the same tired, old mistakes.

Struggling to find some way of legislating or educating or organizing prejudice, greed, jealousy, hate and envy out of the human heart.

Strange, stubborn streak in human make-up . . .

Demanding kingdom of God conditions without kingdom of God men!

Kingdom of God men are not made . . . they are born!

Born by the power of God through the grace that is in Jesus Christ.

Born through the efficacy of the death and resurrection of the Son of God/Son of man!

Born when they acknowledge their sin—turn to God in repentance.

"Unless one is born anew he cannot see the kingdom of God" (John 3:3). "To all who received him [Christ] . . . he gave the power to become the children of God; who were born . . . of God" (John 1:12, 13).

61 — Thanksgiving Is Maturity

". . . or give thanks to him."

Thus the apostle Paul describes the disintegration and degeneration of humanity, self-alienated from God (Rom. 1:21).

In one respect ingratitude is the bottom sin. It speaks of indifference; indifference to the benefits which are so monotonously regular that one takes them for granted: three square meals a day; clean sheets and a pillow; cool fresh water at the turn of a tap. Familiarity inclines a man to contempt, even for the commonplace blessings of life.

Ingratitude speaks of indifference to the wretchedness of others. To be thankless for one's common blessings is to be blind and deaf and dumb to the plight of those who do not have the common blessings to enjoy. Thanklessness is thoughtlessness, carelessness; it is to be casual and aloof when one ought to be concerned and involved. Thanklessness is to live like a vegetable, taking whatever comes with parasitical and selfish indolence, impervious to the tragedy and needs of others.

Ingratitude speaks of indifference to God! Ingratitude is literally godlessness! The thankless person has no sense of God, no sense of manhood, no humility. He is a little country bounded on the north, south, east and west by himself. He is the center and circumference of his little world. He is his own god! He worships himself!

How different thankfulness. The thankful person never stops maturing in heart and life. He respects life, reverences the God whose mercies are new every morning, whose grace sustains perpetually. He enjoys each moment of life; relishes each day with its gifts and benefits, recognizing God as the Giver. Continual thankfulness is the Christian's high road to heaven's bliss here and now!

"Always and for everything giving thanks in the name of our Lord Jesus Christ to God the Father" (Eph. 5:20).

62 — One Way

Truth is always exclusive!

You cannot make a true statement about anything without excluding others—whatever area of life is being discussed.

Two plus two equals four. That excludes three or five. The shortest distance between two points is a straight line. Crooked lines need not apply.

Men are operating on this basis all the time—stating truths which in the nature of things exclude other views.

Error is a fact of life, too . . .

And truth and error are mutually exclusive.

Yet there are those offended by Jesus' statement, "I am the way, and the truth, and the life, no one comes to the Father, but by me."

If Jesus is not the only way to the Father, how many other ways are there?

Or are all ways to the Father true ways?

If not, who decides which are the true ways and which are not?

How bad (or wrong) does a man have to be to miss the way . . . or how good (or right) does a man have to be to make it?

Who decides where the line is drawn between making and missing the way?

Unless you insist that any way is right and true, you eliminate some—and the minute you eliminate any, you are the judge of which ways are to be excluded.

You are guilty of the same narrowness of which you accuse Jesus.

It is just possible that in the effort to broaden the way to God, you actually make it more exclusive than Jesus.

In fact, think it through and see if you can come up with a way less exclusive than Jesus' invitation, "Whosoever will may come."

One can hardly issue a more generous invitation than that. If some condition more than willingness is required, what is that condition to be? Can you think of any condition broader and more inclusive?

". . . the *gift* of God is eternal life." It's free to anyone who will take it!

You can't beat that! Any other way you suggest is more exclusive!

63 — Defeat Is Part of Triumph

"One of the supreme tests of a leader is this—how does he take defeat? Does he take it as final—or does he use it as an educational incident?" ("Tips on Leadership," H. N. Casson, *Forbes Magazine of Business*). Once when Edison was working on an experiment, his discouraged assistant was ready to give up when they had failed for the 1,000th time. Edison persevered. Said he, "We know a thousand things that won't work, let's find one that will." He did! Character, like muscle, must be developed. No one can give it to you anymore than he can give you big muscles. You have to earn it with exercise. Sometimes painful exercise. Defeat is exercise for the character. Take it as a lesson. Don't feel sorry for yourself. Men who take the easy way out are flabby—dull—soft. Men who have learned how to grow by defeat and failure are solid—sharp—hard. They have a cutting edge on their lives. They are the ones that keep business and industry on its feet!

"The biggest club in the world is the 'Down and Out Club.' Most men are brittle. They are like a pitcher that goes to the well, hits a stone and is broken in pieces. Most men start out in life gaily until they hit the first stone. Then they're done for. They might do very well in a world that is filled with cushions, but they are of little value in a world filled with stones" (*Tips on Leadership*). "Too many men get into business life who should never have left the nursery. They go through life snivelling, 'Somebody hit me' " (Casson).

Here is one of the supreme lessons of the Gospel. A man becomes perfect through the things which he suffers. Trials, failures, defeats, season and temper a man. They give elasticity to absorb shock—and come back. Providing, of course, he takes defeats as lessons instead of whimpering with self-pity. No man is good until he has the "whine" knocked out of him! Paul, the apostle, described life as a race. Plenty of men start okay—the champion is the one that finishes . . . even though he gets spiked—or tripped—or "cut out" on a curve.

Business is hard work these days. Sometimes it will seem that everything: government, consumer, labor, management, circumstances are conspiring to keep you from succeeding. That man carries the day who takes every knock—every test—every failure—every defeat as another lesson. Men like this grow—get to be big men under pressure. Christ never promised life without knocks—He did promise strength to keep on keeping on.

"Let us run with perseverance the race that is set before us, looking to Jesus . . ." (Heb. 12:1, 2).

64 – Faith

How does one think of faith?

Do not think of it as buying power—as "coin of the realm" — as a means of exchange of which one has more or less to purchase smaller or larger blessing.

Do not think of faith as a virtue which merits a reward from God . . .

Like a father giving his child a piece of candy for "being a good boy."

Do not think of faith quantitatively — as though it comes in pints and quarts . . . in ounces and pounds.

Think of faith qualitatively . . .

Like openness to a person: You are introduced to a stranger — you hold out your hand — take his — "receive" him at face value.

Think of faith as responding to a person (or any other fact) affirmatively—as over against rejection.

Think of faith as acceptance of that person . . .

Beginning a personal relationship which can be nurtured and developed into a deep friendship.

Think of faith as an accepting—growing—deepening relationship with Jesus Christ.

Jesus Christ makes Himself known through the Bible —through His disciples—in worship.

A personal relationship with Him is nurtured by these same means.

Like a stranger knocking at your front door waiting for you to open and invite him in, Jesus Christ stands at the door of each man's heart, quietly knocking— patiently waiting—for acceptance.

"Behold, I stand at the door and knock; if any one hears my voice and opens the door, I will come in to him and eat with him, and he with me" (Rev. 3:20).

"Faith comes from what is heard, and what is heard comes from the preaching of Christ" (Rom. 10:17).

65 — Christmas Is God's Idea!

Only God could have thought of Christmas!

Christmas is uninventable! No man would ever think to do such a phenomenal thing in such an obscure way. The greatest single event in human history — (paling into oblivion the rise and fall of empires) holding eternal import, ushered in with embarrassing simplicity: stable, manger, lowing oxen, shepherds. It certainly was not a fabrication of man. Man can't do big things in little ways. He is far more inclined to puff up little things; overdo them, build them up out of all proportion to their worth. This is evident in what man tries to make of Christmas. He can't leave this divine event alone in its quiet, unassuming eloquence. He must dress it up, deck it out with tinsel, lights, ribbon, ornaments, frills. And more often than not the central fact of Christmas is lost in the trappings!

This is the danger we all face at Christmas time. It almost seems to get worse year by year. We find ourselves under the weight of the paraphernalia man has invented to clutter up the birthday of the Savior. We get victimized by it, even in the church. Catch ourselves doing everything, not in terms of honoring Christ, but in terms of customs, pressure of advertising propaganda, and often out of sheer selfishness and pride. Gifts, cards, remembrances are given, not for the sake of giving, but in order to escape the humiliation one feels when he receives from one to whom he gives nothing. What a farce! Yet how easily we succumb!

Way out of this caricature of Christmas is not a negative one! It's not a matter of fighting the status quo. It is a matter of giving Christ His proper place in Christmas! When He is exalted, these trappings melt into insignificance. His glory transcends everything else! Try this emphasis this year in heart and home! These other things will be a part of Christmas to be sure, but don't allow them to crowd out Christ from the center of your celebration!

Make room for Him this Christmas! Even though there was no room for Him when He came the first time. Don't relegate Christ to a stable; let your heart be His throne room. Give Him the place of honor at your business and family functions. Adore Him! Worship Him! This can be your best Christmas when you make room for Christ in your plans. He will transform everything about Christmas. Make it scintillate and glow with His radiance! Let Christ be central!

"God so loved the world that he gave his only Son, that whoever believes in him should not perish but have eternal life" (John 3:16).

66 — The Whole Counsel of God

An unbalanced spiritual diet has serious consequences!

Take the man who indulges only in truth which caters to his whims . . . reads only self-pleasing parts of the Bible . . . preoccupies himself with ideas which leave his status quo undisturbed . . . who has no "stomach" for the "whole counsel of God."

"Having itching ears" such a person listens only when the teacher gives him what he enjoys. Let a speaker fail to conform—deviate from the favored line, the ears close and the mind rests. Hearing he hears not, and if the unpleasant theme persists, another teacher is sought.

Like a glutton, he craves to feast on light, rich, pleasant, exotic spiritual morsels . . . and the more predigested, the better.

He doesn't grow strong . . . he just gets spiritually fat—soft—slothful—apathetic.

People like this never join a church . . . they join preachers. They make a career of listening . . . and they become professional critics.

"Preach love," says one. "I don't like judgment." He has no appetite for the strong meat of righteousness—not to mention the fact that he really doesn't understand love. He has sentimentalized it beyond recognition.

Character is the backbone of love . . . and character means virtue. Virtue repudiates unrighteousness—is a consistent judgment upon it.

"The Sermon on the Mount is my religion," says another. By which he generally means some thoughts he has sifted from "The Sermon" which delight his fancy—carefully avoiding hard truth which rebukes his apathy or challenges his status quo. Often in this category is the man who will "take Jesus" but is horrified with the "Christ of Paul." (As though there were a difference.)

"Preach grace," urges another. Works have no place in his appetite. Ephesians is his book (parts of it that is) . . . but away with James. Tell him that a man is saved by grace . . . but don't spoil it by reminding him that grace which saves generates works which become the sons of God.

Announce a series on Daniel or Revelation — the crowd comes. Dig into the ethics of God's Word — discuss the strong meat of man's duty—the crowd thins out perceptibly. "Johnny on the spot" for prophecy—interest lags otherwise.

What a choice vessel unto the Lord is the man who takes the whole Word of God as his counsel — who doesn't flinch when truth penetrates and demands a verdict of personal commitment—who chews patiently the meat of the Word . . . and obeys it! — who "endures hardness as a good soldier of Jesus Christ."

"Every branch of mine that bears no fruit, he takes away . . ." (John 15:2).

67 — Each Man Is Important

There is a kind of indispensability about every man!

In the economy of God every man is meant to be a divine original, unique from all other men, with a distinctive function and purpose in life. Just as God is the Author of infinite variety in lesser things in nature, so the crowning glory of His creation, man, should be marked with this variety. Every snowflake, every blade of grass, every grain of sand, every petal on every flower different; so every human being should bear this stamp of the Creator's originality. (One aspect of sin is this, it is monotonous. Sin leads to boredom, to fed-upness, to tiresome sameness. It keeps a man from being himself.)

The life that is molded by God finds its peculiar place in the world, blending into the total picture, supplementing and complementing other lives, doing its task, fulfilling its purpose to the benefit of all the others and the whole. Like a finely woven tapestry: each thread, each color fulfilling its purpose, indispensable to the design of the artist. The tragedy of course is that the whole picture suffers when one man is ever-so-little out of place, out of line with the plan of the Designer, just as the tapestry suffers when a thread is missing.

Think of the chain reaction of one man out of place. One man out of place, but not just he who suffers. There is the primary effect on his home, his family, his friends, his colleagues, his community; all of them something less than they might be because he is something less than he ought to be. Then the secondary reaction of those who might have been different if the one man's family and friends had been different. So it goes; one man's out of placeness sets in motion reactions that move from him in concentric circles causing immeasurable maladjustment throughout the sphere of his influence directly and indirectly.

Of course life compensates for this maladjustment. Others move in and take up the slack, fill in the gap, but things are not as they might be. Men move in to make the best of the loss of the man out of place, but it is never the same. Trace a tragedy that touches many lives back to its source, and you will often find one man failing to be what he ought to be. Pull a thread out of a tapestry and see the difference. Leave a note out of a melody, a color out of a painting; just one makes the difference! That is why it is imperative and intelligent for a man to give himself to God to be owned and possessed and guided by God, to be molded by God's hand, fashioned into the man he should be—will be—under God's leading.

"I appeal to you therefore . . . by the mercies of God, to present your bodies as a living sacrifice . . . to God, which is your spiritual worship" (Rom. 12:1).

68 — The Real Problem

Accurate diagnosis is fundamental to cure!

However excellent the prescription, it is inadequate for healing if based upon incorrect analysis of the symptoms.

Hence the monotonous, aggravating failure of man's best efforts to solve his problems . . .

His diagnosis is faulty!

Human nature being what it is, and human pride persisting as it does, man refuses to believe anything but the best about himself . . .

Human-like, he blames everything but himself for his trouble. It's the government or education or the law or the Republicans or the Democrats or Jews or Protestants or Catholics or preachers or management or labor or the President or Communism, and so on, ad nauseum!

And man goes on in his blundering, egotistical way, puttering with the symptoms while the disease rages unchecked. The pay-off is precisely what we feel at this mid-twentieth century . . . complete frustration!

"We have harnessed the atom, but we will never make war obsolete until we find a force that will bridle the passions of men and nations," declared General Carlos Romulo of the Philippines, while President of the United Nations.

That's the real problem—the passions of men . . .

"There is nothing outside a man which by going into him can defile him; but the things which come out of a man are what defile him . . . For from within, out of the heart of man, come evil thoughts, fornication, theft, murder, adultery, coveting, wickedness, deceit, licentiousness, envy, slander, pride, foolishness. All these evil things come from within, and they defile the man" (Mark 7:15, 21-23).

The wisest Teacher who ever lived—who knew human nature as no other man — the Great Physician Himself, diagnosed the trouble as a malignancy within the human heart which infects everything man touches!

"Man is his own biggest problem!" For this reason, Jesus Christ came to this world, to offer Himself as the cure for the disease of sin. He did not come just to teach . . . He came to redeem!

"If any one is in Christ, he is a new creation" (2

Cor. 5:17). "I am not ashamed of the gospel: it is the power of God for salvation . . ." (Rom. 1:16).

69 — Salt of the Earth

There are those who are so "heavenly minded they're no earthly good!" Their religion is utterly unlike that of the Lord they profess. The holiness of Jesus worked in actual life! He did not run from the secular; He was immersed in it. His holiness was not for the ivory tower or the sequestered existence, it was for life! It was not for the monastery, it was for the road! The Pharisees could not figure Him. He was a mystery to them. He was continually breaking their religious rules.

Jesus was inconsistent to the religionists of His day, but He was thoroughly consistent with His Father in heaven. Religion to Jesus was not rules, but love: Love for God and love for the needy, the dispossessed, the sick, the sinful, the unholy. Jesus accused the religionists of emptying God's Word of its meaning by "teaching for doctrines the commandments of men." (It is easier to obey rules than to love men.) Pseudo holiness cannot take the wear and tear of daily life. It tries to escape actualities with rules and regulations which help to vindicate its escapism.

In the name of what is miscalled "separation" some isolate themselves from the world and insulate themselves against its sin, leaving an impassable gulf between them and the very people they ought to be loving and helping. Hence the secular man does not take Christians seriously. He has not seen demonstrated a faith that has everyday answers. He is unimpressed with Christians, because their faith seems so irrelevant.

The Pharisees called Jesus a "drunkard, winebibber, glutton." To them He was irreligious, secular, blasphemous. And Jesus would come in for the identical criticism today by some who have managed to lose contact completely with the world God loves and for whom Christ died!

A Christian can escape certain tensions in the conflict between good and evil by running away from the world's burdens, but to do so is to repudiate the authentic Christian way. Love takes the initiative! Love is selfless! Love is not preoccupied with its own whiteness, but with the needy.

"You are the salt of the earth." Salt works on contact, otherwise it is useless. "You are the light of the world." Light was meant to penetrate darkness, not flee it.

70 — Begin With God

A friend writes—"I guess I have a typical case of I believe—but I doubt. I doubt that God is guiding me regarding my future.

"For the past five years my job history has been quite poor — not by my choice, but by circumstances I had little to do with. No doubt my faith has grown with these experiences, but when does it stop?

"Naturally I want some security with a happy job but when does this—if ever—come about? I'm grateful for health—for family—etc., but boy, does it get frustrating regarding this employment thing."

What does one do in such a situation?

He begins by accepting the fact of his circumstances as they are.

One of the hardest things we have to do is accept things as they are . . . but that is the only solid foundation for growth and progress.

We keep trying to build on things as we wish they were . . .

That's like starting to build from the top down.

The dreams keep collapsing.

You cannot begin where you are not!

Wherever you are—however difficult it is—however

adverse the circumstances . . . that's where you must begin . . .

That's where God will begin with you!

The apostle Paul knew the secret . . .

He wrote, "I have learned in whatever state I am, to be content . . . ." He wrote, ". . . by the grace of God I am what I am."

He didn't resign himself to the status quo, nor did he resent reversals. He rejoiced in whatever his circumstances were in the conviction that God was leading.

Favorable circumstances do not necessarily indicate divine favor . . . nor do unfavorable circumstances indicate divine displeasure.

God's promise to lead—despite the circumstances— is all we need. That's the way of faith!

71 – Be Grateful and Grow

Gratitude too is an accurate index to a man's character. The measure of man's thankfulness is one measure of his integrity; for no man rises very high without the help of multitudes of obscure people who love him enough to give him a boost.

In this sense the "self-made" man is a myth. He has simply forgotten, or overlooked, or ignored those who have given him a lift and provided the raw material that went into his success.

The truly great man never struts! He is humbly aware of the unknown and unsung who built into his life the components that led to achievement. The truly great man is a grateful man, and his gratitude shows.

Of course there are little men who have managed to maneuver into places of greatness, but they live in an awful illusion. They strut and preen and gloat. They fancy the attention given them is sincere, whereas it is only the flattery of little men like themselves manipulating for position and favor; who would not hesitate a moment to dethrone the very man they patronize.

The little man lacks assurance, and he demonstrates this by his pig headedness, conceit, ingratitude, belligerence. He's always on the defensive. The sign and seal of his insecurity is his boast that he is "self-made."

Authentic greatness always expresses itself in gratitude! Most of all gratitude to God. The truly great man is aware of the divine favor that has been his from birth, even before birth; which providentially installed him in his position. The man who does not recognize the goodness of God which led to his rise, does not deserve his position and is not qualified to hold it. He may stay there by throwing his weight around, but others yield to his pressure only because they are biding the time until the little tin god will collapse and they can move in and take over!

"For promotion cometh neither from the east, nor from the west, nor from the south. But God is the judge: he putteth down one, and setteth up another" (Psalm 75:6, 7, KJV).

72 — Individual Guilt — and Repentance

Corporate guilt is an illusion!

The only relief is to the one who is imposing it . . . the prophet seems to exclude himself from the indictment.

By blaming everyone else he's home and free . . . his blanket accusation salves his own conscience.

He may even feel he's a hero—daring to take such a bold stand against society in general.

Actually corporate responsibility is meaningless . . .

People feel responsible individually or not at all.

To be sure responsible persons identify with other responsible persons and thus assume responsibility corporately . . .

But as soon as individuals within such a collective

lose their sense of responsibility the whole structure weakens.

The only ones who take corporate guilt seriously are those who suffer personal guilt . . . those not bothered by personal guilt couldn't care less.

Corporate guilt gives them a perfect opportunity to cop out!

For the thoughtful person there's no way out from corporate guilt. He may regret his failure—his prejudice—his sin—and attempt to do something about it . . . but he finds no relief for the prophet of doom—painting everybody with the same brush—includes him in his relentless blanket condemnation.

God promises to forgive and bless a repentant nation . . . but repentance itself is a one-by-one proposition.

Apart from individual repentance there is no corporate forgiveness and renewal.

Persisting in the accusation of corporate guilt finally immobilizes a society because there is no way for the individual to respond and there is no other way society can respond to any challenge except individually.

Perpetrating social guilt is futile!

"If my people who are called by my name humble themselves, and pray and seek my face, and turn from their wicked ways, then I will hear from heaven, and will forgive their sin and heal their land" (2 Chron. 7:14).

73 — The Sacrifice of Praise

Try spending a week praising God every day as often as you remember. Let your prayers be nothing but praise and thanksgiving to God for one week! Praise Him for past blessings, the good things He has done, things long since forgotten, but for which you were thrillingly grateful at the time.

Praise Him for health and strength, which you've

taken for granted, as though you keep your heart pumping seventy-five times a minute, as though you operate the bellows that suck clean oxygen in, drive wastes out. Praise God for the remarkable body He gave you!

Praise God for His keeping power day in, day out, year after year.

Praise Him for the sunshine, the rain, the clouds, the cool breezes, the heat, the brooks and streams and rivers and lakes and oceans. Praise Him for the mountains, the valleys, the grass and trees and flowers, the birds and animals and fish. Praise Him for the fabulous beauty He has lavished upon the world for you; the bountiful resources He put here for you to enjoy and develop.

Praise God for your family, your neighbors and friends. Praise Him for your job, for your superiors, your colleagues, your subordinates. Praise Him for work to do, for responsibility, for duty.

Praise Him for clean sheets between which to sleep, for three square meals a day. Praise Him for plenty and for want; for supply and for need; for prosperity and poverty. Praise Him for the unexpected; the planned; the delights; the disappointments.

Praise God for danger and difficulty; for testing, trials and tragedy; for hazards and hurdles; for obstacles that season and temper you; for competition that exercises your faith and builds muscle in your character, and keeps you from getting soft and lazy and complacent.

Praise Him for the trouble that knocks whine and self-pity out of you, that puts a cutting edge on your life, makes you sharp, alert, sensitive, on your toes.

Most of all praise God for Himself! For His love; His mercy; His grace; His goodness; His justice; His integrity; His perfection! Praise God because He is!

Offer God the "sacrifice of praise." That is, praise Him when you don't feel like it; when circumstances are dead against you. Praise Him because you know that however you feel, whatever the circumstances, God is God, eternally perfect, unchanging, unimpeachable.

Praise Him for His Son; the cross; the resurrection, and the sure promise of His coming again. Praise God that the ultimate triumph of Christ in history is absolutely certain! That "every knee shall bow—and every tongue confess that Jesus Christ is Lord!" That the kingdoms of this world shall become the kingdoms of our Lord and of His Christ!

Praise God! For one solid week, every time you think to do it!

"In everything God works for good with those who love him, who are called according to his purpose" (Rom. 8:28).

74 — Ask — and Receive

Some things come only by prayer!

It is not accurate to say, "It will happen whether we pray or not."

In many specifics, God waits to be asked.

Naturally there are many blessings of God which are given without respect to the one who receives them . . .

Rain falls upon the just and the unjust . . . the sun shines upon a man's fields whether he is good or wicked . . .

But in many of the specific blessings of life, the heavenly Father waits to be asked before He bestows them.

Having made man a free moral agent, with a sovereign will of his own, God will not violate man's freedom by imposing upon him that which the man does not want.

Therefore in many of the personal blessings of life, God gives as man requests.

And He will not give if man does not ask!

Prayer, rightly understood, is an integral part of man's relationship to God. By prayer man exposes himself to God's will—opens his heart to the wisdom of the heavenly Father—submits himself to the divine purpose.

Prayer is not just getting things from God—though there is that aspect to it . . . it is consenting to God—yielding to God — once God's will has been made known through prayer.

Blessings falling upon a man whether he wants them or not may turn out to be a curse.

Getting accustomed to the good things, he is inclined to treat them with contempt . . . taking them for granted, he grows indifferent to the Giver.

"The goodness of God leads to repentance . . ." Therefore, blessings of God—received whether he asks for them or not—coming with commonplace regularity —may be the very things which condemn a man.

Indifferent to the Giver—he does not repent—and piles up judgment against himself.

In the economy of God the richest benefits of heaven are reserved for those who want them—who ask for them.

"You do not have, because you do not ask!" (James 4:2). "Ask and you shall receive!" (Jesus).

75 – The Strategy of Waiting

Sometimes the most important thing a man can do is wait! It is the most difficult but often by far the wisest strategy.

God's will involves a schedule as well as a purpose to be accomplished. Submission to His schedule is as important as submission to His purpose.

Timing in anything is basic. Take cooking for instance: The good chef takes time seriously. He doesn't want a half-baked product! (He doesn't leave a thing in the oven too long either.) Whether it's cooking or comedy; drama or real life; timing is fundamental. Acting on impulse is wrong; failing to act because of fear is just as wrong! The balance is learning to wait on God, to let God lead. He will!

The impulsive man gets an idea, runs off with it in all directions, leaves behind a string of half-baked projects. Disregarding divine guidance he whips up a storm, gets things in motion, then lets them peter out. He majors in starting things; fails at the finish, and leaves life cluttered up with a lot of loose ends. He calls it faith; but he's really operating on presumption.

Just as bad is the lazy, or fearful, or faithless man who never starts anything (he figures he can't fail if he doesn't try), and lets ideas burn out to ashes.

The man who waits on God enjoys the perfection of divine timing and completion. Question is when does a man wait? how long does he wait? what tips him off to action?

First thing to remember is that when God gives a vision, God Himself will fulfill it! He will use the man, but God by His Holy Spirit is the animation, the dynamic. The man who waits for God to act in him will be the most active, the most involved in the operation. God may use many different means to guide a man, but in the final analysis the guidance is inward, intuitive. By His indwelling Spirit God frees or binds, releases or checks. The man who waits on God becomes sensitive to the "inner voice." Got a good idea? Think it is born of God? Give it back to Him; wait reflectively, prayerfully, quietly. (You never waste any time waiting on God!) As long as there is doubt, don't!

"Commit your way to the Lord; trust in him, and he will act" (Ps. 37:5). "Let steadfastness have its full effect" (James 1:4).

103

God has not abdicated!

The agony of our time is evidence of the accuracy of the Bible's statements concerning the last days . . .

And a mark of the nearness of the return of Jesus Christ!

The space race—the mad rush to stockpile atomic weapons — the frustration and futility of diplomacy — the unpredictable eruption of trouble spots like pus sacks—the increase of social tension—the acceleration of crime and festering social malignancy — the hot breath of nationalism and revolution — the sickening, unrelenting inexorable threat of thermo-nuclear war . . .

These are not the death rattle of Christian civilization . . . they are the birth pangs of Christian fulfillment!

Universal trouble does not spell doom . . . it proclaims victory!

"The whole creation is on tiptoe to see the wonderful sight of the sons of God coming into their own. The world of creation cannot as yet see reality . . . yet it has been given hope. And the hope is that in the end the whole of created life will be rescued from the tyranny of change and decay, and have its share in that magnificent liberty which can only belong to the children of God!

"It is plain to anyone with eyes to see that at the present time all created life groans in a sort of universal travail . . . while we wait for that redemption of our bodies which will mean that at last we have realized our full sonship in him" (Rom. 8:19-23, Phillips).

Scoffers mock at the thought of Christ's return on the grounds that the Church has waited for this event for nineteen centuries . . . and this very scoffing fulfills Bible prediction . . . it is one of the signs (2 Pet. 3:3-5).

Nothing is more certain than Christ's triumphal reentry into history . . . and it's 1900 years nearer than when it was first promised!

Today the whole universe languishes for the return of the Prince of Peace.

". . . and the kingdoms of this world shall become the kingdoms of our Lord and of his Christ."

77 – Prayer and Forgiveness

Many of us pray the prayer once a week . . .

And if God answers prayer (which He does) . . . the evil consequences are incalculable.

". . . forgive us our trespasses as we forgive those who trespass against us."

That's the prayer — part of the so-called "Lord's Prayer" which many of us pray as we worship weekly.

If God answers that prayer—what incredible judgment upon some . . .

For they simply refuse to forgive those who trespass against them!

It is no wonder the church has lost its power . . .

No wonder faith is unreal . . .

No wonder the large majority of Americans (according to a recent poll) consider the Christian religion irrelevant.

If God forgives as we forgive . . . and that is what we are asking Him to do when we pray that prayer . . .

How many of us live in broken relationship with God?

When Jesus taught the "Lord's Prayer," He lifted from it that one petition, as if to say, this is crucial.

He said quite plainly, "If you do not forgive men their trespasses, neither will your Father forgive you your trespasses."

In other words, you can't be right with God if you're not right with others.

Which was the point of his instruction, "If you are offering your gift at the altar, and there remember that your brother has something against you, leave your gift . . . *first* be reconciled to your brother, and then come and offer your gift" (Matt. 5:23, 24).

Reconciliation demands priority!

Undoubtedly the explanation for much of the deadness in Christian experience is due to our refusal to be reconciled.

There is nothing important until you have done that!

78 — The Peril of Secularism

The reason why some men crack up is that they have nothing inside to take up the shock! Nothing to resist the pressure, no resiliency, no inner resources to depend on! Outwardly they seem strong, masculine, powerful; you would think nothing could overcome them, but inside, where it really matters when the going is tough, they have nothing! They are hollow, empty, dried up! Like an egg shell with the insides sucked out, dried up, they crumble under pressure. They go to pieces, there is nothing holding them together inside, no body, no substance.

There is a place in a man's life only God can fill! There is a "God-shaped vacuum" in every man. No one else, nothing else will do, only God. No substitutes will satisfy. The Bible puts it this way: ". . . [going] after worthlessness, and became worthless" (Jer. 2:5). Someone has paraphrased it this way: "Following after hollow gods, they became hollow souls." There are three basic principles in that statement of Jeremiah, three characteristics of human nature, three laws of life.

The first—man is incurably religious! If he does not follow the true God, he must find a substitute. This is confirmed over and over in men. They become religious about many other things than God. Sometimes atheists are most religious! Atheism is a faith! The atheist has faith that there is no God. He believes in "No-god"! It takes a lot of faith to believe that way;

against all the evidence. Second — there is something in man's nature which inclines him away from the true God to substitutes. Something in man that makes him follow idols. Something which makes him worship creature instead of Creator. He makes his god, instead of letting God make him! Third—man becomes like the god he follows. Following hollow gods, he becomes a hollow soul. This is inevitable; the inexorable law of man's inner nature, his soul.

Men have let money become their god and have become hard, cold, metallic like their money. Or they have made power their god and become thoughtless, indifferent, cruel, inhuman, animalistic. Some have made pleasure their god and become shallow, giddy, empty, foolish! To others popularity or fame is god. It turns them into cocky, conceited, heady, stuffed-shirts. When these substitutes for God rule the life, it takes more and more of them to give less and less satisfaction. Until a man gets weary, bored, fed up!

When God rules the life, it becomes more and more satisfying, more and more meaningful, more and more livable, increasingly more productive. And at man's center is stability, strength, poise, rebound from any shock, any pressure.

"Turn from idols to serve the living and true God!"

"But whosoever drinks of the water that I shall give him will never thirst; the water that I shall give him will become in him a spring of water welling up to eternal life" (John 4:14).

79 — Take Time

Time for God . . . time with God . . .
One of the essential priorities in the Seventies!
You don't have time . . .
You must find time—take time—make time!
Time to talk with God . . .
Time to listen to God . . .

Time to wait on God—to get God's point of view—to think God's thoughts.

Get a modern version of the Bible: J. B. Phillips—New English—etc. Even if you read the Authorized without difficulty — familiarity with favorite passages prevents you from seeing them afresh.

Set aside a period when you can be alone—preferably early in the morning—schedule this as your daily rendezvous with God.

It is a time for the open heart and mind as you read the Bible—think about what you read—seek its application that day in your life—and commit your way to God for the day.

Let prayer be conversation with God—sharing your thoughts — your concerns — your needs — your hopes and aspirations — your burdens for the family, the job, and others.

Think of yourself as being God's servant for that day —an instrument in His hands for His work—a garment He wears to do what He wills wherever He leads you.

Then go with God!

"Blessed is the man who walks not in the counsel of the wicked, nor stands in the way of sinners, nor sits in the seat of scoffers; but his delight is in the law of the Lord, and on his law he meditates day and night. He is like a tree planted by streams of water, that yields its fruit in its season, and its leaf does not wither. In all that he does, he prospers" (Ps. 1:1-3).

80 – The God Mammon

The most exacting test of man's character is money!

What a man does with his money, or what he lets his money do to him, is the most precise, sharp, illuminating index into his real self. Men have made lots of money and have never used it at all! They let it use them. They thought they were making it; in reality it was making them. And when money makes a man, it destroys him! This is one of the pitiful tragedies in life—the men who began by mastering money and ended by letting money master them.

Money can become an idol in a man's life easier than any other single thing. It can take God's place in your life more quickly than anything else if you are not careful. That is the reason why Jesus Christ spoke so much about money. Not that He was interested in it for its own sake, but He was gravely concerned with the force, the power, the havoc it could play in a man's life.

You see a man need not have money for it to wreck him. It can ruin a man when he doesn't have a cent! Once in a conversation with His disciples, Jesus made this startling statement: "It is harder for a rich man to enter the kingdom of heaven than for a camel to go through the eye of a needle." That was a staggering thing to say, but the reaction of His disciples was even more alarming. They said, "Who then can be saved?" If a rich man can't be saved, then nobody can! that was the gist of their question. The Lord responded with two answers: First, "With man it is impossible, but with God all things are possible." Second, not riches themselves, but trust in riches is the enemy of man's soul. Who trusts in money is in the danger zone.

There are really only two kinds of people as far as money is concerned: those who have it, and those who wish they did. In either case, whether a man has it or not, money can be the most important thing in his life. In fact, often the man who has little or no money puts the most importance on it; and when money is the most important thing in a man's life it is the most dangerous thing. Trust in riches is a deceitful, deadly enemy of men's souls.

Not your money, or lack of money, is the important thing; but your attitude toward it. That is the clue to the kind of man you are. Either money is a blessing or it is a curse in your life. Handle it God's way, it is

109

a blessing. Let it handle you, it proves in the end a curse! It will destroy you!

"Man's life does not consist in the abundance of his possessions." "Seek first his kingdom" (Jesus Christ in Luke 12:15, 31).

81 ~ God's Gift

God's answer is a Person!

Theological propositions — philosophical theories — moral precepts will not save man . . .

History is replete with the failure of these—and un-numbered other human inventions and innovations.

God's Gift was a Person—not a theological, philosophical or ethical system.

God's Gift was His Son!

God's Gift was Himself in His Son . . .

God's Gift was incarnation!

God's total answer to man's total need is Jesus Christ!

No one ever tried Jesus Christ—whatever his need—and found Him inadequate.

Never has a man related personally to Jesus Christ and been disappointed.

Many have embraced a religious system called Christianity and found it inadequate . . .

Many have joined an institution called the church and found it irrelevant . . .

Many have been enamored of theological, philosophical and ethical schemes only to be disenchanted and disillusioned.

Many have adopted rules of piety and rebelled.

No man has trusted Jesus Christ vainly!

This is the heart of Christmas—God loved man and as the supreme expression of that love, sent His Son into the world to cure the sickness of the world.

Obviously Jesus Christ cannot work in a man's life if that man will not personally accept Him—anymore than medication will work if it is not applied.

Christmas is for you! It will be the greatest day of your life . . . if you will receive the Gift of gifts, God's only Son.

82 — The Choice Is Yours

One of the most important life strategies is to realize that nothing can really hurt you unless you allow it to. Troubles and trials, reverses and tragedy come to every man. Rare is the man, and usually half-baked, who escapes the trials and tribulations in life.

But it is how a man takes trouble that makes the difference between ruin and reconstruction in his life.

To illustrate: Here is a man who is visited with some great tragedy unexpectedly. It bowls him over. He turns bitter and sour, complains, blames God for his trouble, asks "Why did this have to happen to me?" He hardens his heart to those about Him and to God. What this man is doing is allowing the tragedy to do irreparable damage in his life. It is not just the thing that happened to him; it is the way he acts after it happens that is really destroying him.

Here is another man with just as great tragedy, just as unexpectedly. He cannot understand why this thing happened the way it did, when it did; the whole mess does not make sense to him, but he softens his heart toward God. He believes that God is able to take the tragedy and turn it into victory in his life. Instead of turning bitter and hardened, he turns sweet and mature. He is allowing himself to be seasoned by the trouble. Actually he will be a better man than if the trouble had not come. By taking difficulty with a heart warm and soft toward God, by turning to Him in the midst of a problem, a man will discover that the thing that happened to him will make him, not wreck him.

At the bottom it is a matter of sheer choice. Each man decides whether or not he is going to let trouble lick him or make it strengthen him.

Important thing to remember is this: that no matter how a man reacts to trouble, he does not change the fact of trouble. Getting bitter and sour and hard will not alter the fact that trouble has come. Neither will it be altered by a softening of the heart to God, but the point is this: how a man takes what happens to him determines whether that thing will make him or break him. The choice is up to you each time!

"Beloved, do not be surprised at the fiery ordeal which comes upon you to prove you, as though some thing strange were happening to you. But rejoice, so far as you share Christ's sufferings, that you may also rejoice and be glad when his glory is revealed" (1 Pet. 4:12, 13).

83 — The Task of the Church

It is hardly worthwhile to talk about God's love if one does not demonstrate that love in his life!

In fact, to speak of the love of God when one's life does not show this love, can be devastating in its effect upon others . . .

Perhaps no single thing has alienated more people from Christ and the Church than loveless conduct on the part of professing Christians.

The apostle Paul makes it quite clear that without love everything else is futile and meaningless. Without love, eloquence—sacrifice — philanthropy — prophecy (preaching)—discernment—martyrdom—faith—mean nothing at all. They are hollow—transparent—counterfeit—if they are not mixed with love.

God's love is expressed many different ways in the world: in the work of healing done by medical missions at home and abroad—works of charity among orphans, widows, the blind, deaf, dumb and diseased—in education and agriculture . . .

But important as all these are in demonstrating God's love, there is another task which is primary to the Christian—and which is supremely expressive of the love of God—that is the task of evangelism!

By evangelism is meant the telling of the good news (Gospel) that God loved man so much He sent His Son into the world to die for man's sin on the cross. This is the heart of Christian love as evidenced by the golden text of the Bible (John 3:16).

It is good news because it provides man the one possibility to break with his sin. And sin is at the bottom of all of man's problems. It is not how man is organized in social units that is his basic problem . . . but that because of his sin, man will exploit any social organization for his own selfish purposes.

Upset the status quo—by whatever means—and establish a new order . . . man will soon subvert the new order—his sin will soon infect the new order with inequity, injustice and dispeace. This is history!

The Gospel is God's answer to that fundamental issue—human selfishness and greed—human pride and avarice—man's insatiable desire to do as he pleases.

Hence the first missionary, the apostle Paul, traveled throughout the Roman empire preaching the Gospel. In three journeys around the then civilized world, the great apostle plunged into the metropolitan areas armed with one thing—a message!

He spent a year and a half in the most wicked city of his time, Corinth, teaching that Jesus was the Messiah, that He had to suffer and die by crucifixion and be raised from the dead. He understood this to be "the power of God for salvation to every one who has faith."

This is the central and primary mission of the church. Failing in this, it fails ultimately in all others.

84 — Faith in No-god

"Back in the nineteenth century, when atheism was a fad and atheistic lectures drew large crowds, a well-known atheist challenged an equally well-known minister in a debate . . . . The minister set these terms: 'I will come to the debate with 100 persons whose lives have been changed by Jesus Christ. They will give evidence and you may cross-examine them. All I ask is that you bring an equal number of men and women who have been helped by atheism.' The atheist backed down. The debate was never held. The Christian had all the witnesses" (David H. Scott in *Faith At Work* magazine, May-June 1962).

Keeping the discussion at the level of the theoretical and academic, a man can put up a rather convincing argument for atheism. Bring the discussion down to cases; his argument collapses! It may stimulate the ego to believe in "no-god" as long as it's a purely intellectual matter, but get down to live issues, faith in "no-god" can't carry its own weight.

What are the benefits of atheism? With what resources does it endow a man to face life's realities? What has atheism done for the head-hunting aborigine in the mountains of Formosa or the Indian in the hinterland of Ecuador? What does atheism offer the derelict on skid-row, the alcoholic, the estranged husband and wife, the father whose daughter has been "hooked" on drugs? How does atheism help the mother when her child is struck down in traffic, the husband whose beloved has been committed to a mental hospital? What hope does atheism hold for the man who has come to the end of the line, frustrated by his own failure and sin? What is atheism's way out when life tumbles in?

Atheism doesn't care! Sees no intrinsic value in man! Atheism is never constructive. It is totally negative and destructive. It may be interesting to debate with nothing at stake; it is less than useless when the chips are down, a clever theory with no practical value.

"Following hollow gods they became hollow souls" (Jer. 2:5, KJV).

85 — Nothing Just Happens

". . . everything ultimately makes sense."

Such certainty is the "prerogative of the Christian"!

He enjoys . . . "confidence that everything ultimately makes sense."

Nothing just happens!

The God of the Bible: The God of Abraham, Isaac and Jacob—the God of Moses and Joshua and Gideon —the God of Isaiah and Jeremiah—the God of our Lord and Savior Jesus Christ is one and the same!

He is the Author of history.

He is the Lord of history.

He is in charge!

Nothing escapes His notice — nothing is not under His control.

He is the God of the macrocosm . . . He is the God of the microcosm.

He orders the infinite . . . . and the infinitesimal.

Nations do not rise without His providence . . .

Sparrows do not fall without His knowledge.

He knows the end from the beginning—and all the way in between.

We get confused because we are involved in the process—see history from within, as it is evolving rather than at its close.

In those completed parts of history where we have hindsight, we appreciate how circumstances, which in the process looked black, turn out all for the good.

When history has been consummated, then we shall see how perfectly all things worked out—how meaningful every detail was.

Meanwhile we place our confidence in the God of history—who works in history with perfect knowledge, perfect love, perfect justice, perfect control.

Self-sacrifice may be a waste!

". . . simply a disease of the nerves, a morbid self-consciousness which is the obverse of intense selfishness."

The integrity of self is basic to the second great commandment . . .

"Thou shalt love thy neighbor as thyself."

Some men can't love others — *because they do not love themselves.*

They're continually taking self-hate out on others.

Or they pride themselves on their humility.

("How do you help a conceited man when the essence of his conceit is that he is humble?")

Self-abnegation becomes a substitute for Christian character and service.

The remedy is out and out submission to Jesus Christ.

I do not give myself up . . . I give up my right to myself to Christ.

I take self off the throne of my life and invite Christ to reign there.

He is made Lord and King.

Self is elevated to the position of servant of the Most High God.

Christ becomes the center of life — the magnetic north.

Christ becomes the benevolent tyrant.

In losing oneself for the sake of Christ, one finds himself.

"To obey is better than sacrifice."

87 ~ Watch Your Convictions

"Foolish consistency is the hobgobblin of little minds" (Anon).

Religious consistency can be diabolical!

Devotion to God and consistency to religious conviction are not identical.

Consistency to religious conviction may produce a fanatic . . .

Devotion to God will produce a saint!

The Son of God was the most inconsistent Man who ever lived by the standards of the Pharisees. He was continually breaking their rules — continually in hot water with the religionists of His day.

Because they were doggedly consistent to their convictions . . . He was utterly devoted to God's will.

Their convictions had become a fetish. They no longer held their convictions — *their convictions held them!* Their godliness was hollow . . . it possessed the form—but was without power.

The fresh, honest, God-devoted life of Jesus was utterly enigmatic to them. By their standards, Jesus was not only a blasphemer—He was dangerous!

Their religious convictions had become their god. They were idol worshipers as much as the Greek pagans who had altars to every conceivable deity . . . even an altar to "the unknown god."

Their idol was their dogma!

God had been expelled from their religion. They gave Him lip service but their hearts were far from Him.

In fact, their religion had become the enemy of God. Their convictions made them hostile to God's way.

Whatever their excuse—their religion was the reason they crucified Jesus.

And religious conviction has been crucifying Christ in every generation since. Religious conviction is continually nailing righteousness to a cross!

This does not mean that authentic devotion is without dogmatic substance . . . but it does mean that one never equates his doctrinal position with Almighty God. Doctrine, essential as it is, remains subordinate to the Person of Christ.

"Why do you call me Lord, and do not do the things I say?" (Jesus Christ).

88 — Be a Good Neighbor

We think of our peer as our neighbor . . .

And assume a right relation to him fulfills the second great commandment.

Hence the church begins to take on an upper middle class bias . . .

And entrenchment of the status quo deepens.

Gravitating to those of like mind (and like economic status), we scratch each other's back . . .

Collaborate on protecting our interests. . .

And think of this as love of neighbor—

Than which nothing could be further from the truth!

As vividly illustrated by our Lord's response to the lawyer when he defensively asked Jesus, "Who is my neighbor?"

Jesus' reply was the story of the good Samaritan— familiar to all.

Point of the story was not to define "neighbor" for the lawyer . . .

But to show him *he must be a good neighbor* . . .

Especially of the man in need.

He must be neighbor to a stranger . . .

If that stranger is in need.

In the context of the story, one's neighborly responsibility extended to anyone in trouble.

Geographic, cultural, political, social or economic affinity have nothing to do with neighborliness for the Christian.

It transcends all man-made divisions and boundaries and classes and systems.

To love one's neighbor is to respond to the man in need!

"You shall love the Lord your God . . . and your

neighbor as yourself. On these two commandments depend all the law and the prophets" (Matt. 22:37-40).

89 — Slave — Or Free?

How does a man use his freedom?
That is the deepest issue in history!
It has its roots in the garden of Eden.
Despite all his talk about liberty, man consistently uses his freedom in such a way that it leads to slavery.
He begins an act in the name of freedom . . .
Allows it to become a habit which enslaves.
Then agonizes in the struggle to break its shackles.
He acquires possessions for his use . . .
Then gets "hooked" on possessions.
He no longer needs them for use . . .
He needs them for the sake of having them.
He is slave to things.
The tyrants are legion which entice man with the promise of liberty . . .
Only to make him their slave.
Pleasure—status—wealth—position—recognition—all are tyrants which beckon with the promise of independence—then bind with cords of steel.
Self is the chief tyrant—using all other tyrants to get its own way.
"You belong to the power which you choose to obey, whether you choose sin, whose reward is death, or God, obedience to whom means the reward of righteousness" (Rom. 6:16, Phillips).
"Jesus said, 'Believe me when I tell you that every man who commits sin is a slave. . . . if the Son, then, sets you free, you are really free!' " (John 8:36, Phillips).

Boil it down to the real issue, either you come to Jesus —or you go along with His enemies!

That's putting it on the line, but a man ought to level with himself in this matter. No man is more self-deluded than the one who has found a neat compromise on Jesus.

Fuzzy thinking about God comes so easily, if a man bothers to think at all—and a mental jolt helps to get him on balance spiritually.

Complacency is exceedingly subtle when it comes to a man's attitude toward Jesus . . .

Comfortable in his position, he tends to reject automatically anything that disturbs the status quo — his mental reflexes register negative.

Thinking is hard work—so he coasts intellectually—occasionally reorganizes his prejudices — thinks he's thinking—and relaxes.

With the inevitable result that he becomes a bigot—and calls it conviction . . . or an intellectual jellyfish—and calls it tolerance.

But whatever he calls it, the point is that he's lining up with the worst scoundrels of history when he takes a stand against Jesus.

What reasonable explanation is there for rejection of Jesus? Why should anyone turn against a perfect Man and go along with the crowd that liquidated Him?

Three classes of men had a part in his crucifixion: those who engineered it — those who yielded to their pressure . . . and those who just didn't care.

The men who let it happen were as culpable as those who made it happen.

Indifference to Jesus Christ not only constitutes rejection of Him and support of His opposition—it involves the loss of eternal benefits which God offers . . . it is in fact, rejection of the Father.

Jesus said, "If God were your Father, you would love me . . ." (John 8:42).